BAKING YOU HAPPY

The following photographs are courtesy of Shutterstock Images:
p. 14: © Igor Kovalchuk, p. 15: © Nataliia Pyzhova, p. 17: © librakv, p. 18: © hanabiyori, p. 137: © Alison Hancock

Published by Peter Pauper Press, Inc.
202 Mamaroneck Avenue
White Plains, New York 10601
U.S.A.

Published in the United Kingdom and Europe by Peter Pauper Press, Inc.
c/o White Pebble International
Unit 2, Plot 11 Terminus Rd.
Chichester, West Sussex PO19 8TX, UK

Designed by Heather Zschock

Library of Congress Cataloging-in-Publication Data

Lubert, Allison.
  Baking you happy : gluten-free recipes from sweet freedom bakery / by Allison Lubert ;
photographs by Rachel McGinn.
     pages cm
  Includes index.
  ISBN 978-1-4413-1571-7 (pbk. : alk. paper) 1. Gluten-free diet--Popular works. 2.
Gluten-free diet--Recipes. I. Title.
  RM237.86.L83 2014
  641.81'5--dc23
                    2014010922

ISBN 978-1-4413-1571-7
Manufactured for Peter Pauper Press, Inc.
Printed in China

7 6 5 4 3 2 1

Visit us at www.peterpauper.com

BAKING YOU HAPPY

GLUTEN-FREE RECIPES FROM

Sweet Freedom Bakery

gluten-free • vegan • dairy-free • egg-free • soy-free
corn-free • peanut-free • refined-sugar-free

by ALLISON LUBERT

photographs by RACHEL McGINN

PETER PAUPER PRESS
White Plains, New York

This book is dedicated to my wonderful husband,
and greatest taste-tester, Jonathan. You not only encouraged
me to bring my recipes to life via Sweet Freedom Bakery,
but you have advised me and supported the business every step
of the way since we opened our doors. A true partner in every
sense of the word you are, and I can't wait to see what the
future brings for us, and our growing family! I love you.

Table of Contents

Introduction

Sweet Freedom Bakery is proud to be a retail bakery where *all* of the products are free of gluten, dairy, eggs, soy, peanuts, corn, refined-sugars and artificial ingredients. We are 100% vegan and kosher to boot. We pride ourselves on being a safe haven for those with food allergies or celiac disease, as well as those who follow a vegan lifestyle or other special diet. Since our opening in 2010, we have baked our desserts fresh every morning to cater to our appreciative customers who either can't find anywhere to buy that special treat or birthday cake that meets their dietary needs, or who simply want a delicious dessert that tastes like the "normal" gluten- , dairy- , and white-sugar-laden treats that they grew up eating and loving.

Since opening in 2010, business at Sweet Freedom has been booming. We opened our doors with roughly ten recipes and treats to offer, and have grown to expand not only our customer base, but our hours, offerings, and flavors. We have enjoyed praise from local press, positive reviews both online and in person, awards and accolades, and appearances on the *Food Network* and the *Cooking Channel*. It is well-known and documented that food allergies and intolerances are becoming ever more mainstream, and that an increase in the general awareness of how our diet impacts our health and well-being is growing at a rapid pace. We feel proud and lucky to serve an important and growing need in our community. Now it is time to reach more people and bring our coveted recipes into the homes of those around the country.

The most common question we've received from our fans and customers (or anyone who has heard of us) is, "How do you do it?" When they hear that all of our products are free of gluten, dairy, eggs, soy, peanuts, corn, refined-sugars, etc., it is assumed that the taste, texture, or variety of our products will suffer. Once they take one bite of our treats, those concerns are put to rest. In fact, many of our customers don't have a special dietary need or restriction, but simply want a dessert that will taste delicious while not leaving them feeling that sugar "slump" or guilt. We love seeing the looks of surprise and appreciation on the faces of our customers. Many of our fans have tried themselves to create such allergen-free desserts at home to no avail.

This leads us to the second most common question that we've received from customers, which is, "When will your cookbook be available?" Because our recipes took so long to develop, and involved such trial-and-error over months and years, we have been hesitant to put our secrets out there. We realize that it is not only next to impossible to create what we have, but it also requires an intricate understanding of health and nutrition, food chemistry and safety, baking skills, and a ton of patience. This is why there aren't many others out there doing what we are doing. However, as our online sales have begun to grow, and the countless calls and emails that we receive begging for recipe disclosure continue to come in, we realize that it is time to share our methods with everyone. The ingredients that we use and buy in bulk from specific purveyors are now more readily available to the public, and the idea that we can bring a freedom so sweet to more people in their own homes is enticing and exciting.

We know that **Baking You Happy** will give many who need it the flexibility and option to bake our special desserts at home for years to come.

Enjoy! And if you need extra treats or just additional goodies for baking inspiration, remember that we ship nationwide *(see our ordering and contact information on page 143)*.

Happy baking,

Allison Lubert

Owner of Sweet Freedom Bakery

About the Author

Allison Lubert received her Bachelor's degree from Tufts University and holds a Master's degree in Psychological Services as well as an advanced Master's in Professional Counseling & Psychology from the University of Pennsylvania. Upon completing her graduate coursework and clinical internship, Allison's long-time interest in health and nutrition began to develop further as she struggled with several food allergies, depleted energy, and a weakened immune system. Reading every book on nutrition that she could get her hands on, she developed a deeper appreciation for the way in which food can deeply affect our physical and mental health.

It was then that Allison found a way of eating and living that brought her satisfaction and fulfillment. She continued her studies by enrolling in the Institute for Integrative Nutrition in New York City, an affiliate of Columbia University. Allison then combined her background in counseling, her vast knowledge of dietary theory, and her passion for helping others, to create her private nutritional counseling practice, Apple-A-Day Counseling.

Throughout the time that Allison was completing her education and beginning her nutritional counseling practice, she spent hours in the kitchen experimenting and developing recipes that would accommodate her allergies to wheat and dairy. She is thrilled that this work has come to fruition through the success of Sweet Freedom Bakery, Philadelphia's first and only gluten-free, vegan, allergy-friendly retail bakery. Allison has been excited to provide the best-tasting, allergen-free treats that even those without special diets will love!

Allison lives with her husband, Jonathan, a son, and twin daughters in the Philadelphia suburbs. An avid cook and baker, you will often find her in the kitchen experimenting with ways to make her growing family their favorite foods that are more healthful and flavorful.

STOCKING YOUR
SWEET FREEDOM PANTRY

Ingredients, Tips, & Resources

Please read this section closely before beginning to bake any Sweet Freedom desserts. There is *vital, specific information* on which ingredients to use, why we use them, and where to find them! Also check out our **Approved Sweet Freedom Bakery Suppliers** list *(see page 136)* on how to locate the brands that we recommend (you'll see them mentioned here).

Agave Nectar—Agave nectar is the sweet sap derived from the cactus plant. It is a low-glycemic, natural sweetener that resembles honey in color and texture. We recommend that you use an organic, unrefined version of agave nectar, just as we do at Sweet Freedom, to ensure that it is gentlest on your body and blood sugar levels. **Organic Nectars** is a great brand, and the one that we order in bulk at Sweet Freedom.

Apple Cider Vinegar—Apple cider vinegar is known in the holistic health world as being a cure-all for many ailments. For our purposes in baking, the apple cider vinegar counteracts with the baking soda in our recipes to produce a chemical reaction that makes carbon dioxide and causes our batters to rise and turn out fluffy. We use **Bragg** brand at the bakery, and incorporate it into many of our recipes. Whoever said allergen-free baking wasn't like a science experiment was mistaken!

Apples—At Sweet Freedom we love our apples! You'll find them in many of our goodies, especially in the fall. We try to use organic apples whenever possible and available, and we recommend a mixture of tart and sweet apples to give a nice flavor profile to whatever you're baking.

Applesauce—Applesauce has a big job at Sweet Freedom. It is an often crucial replacement for eggs, helps to bind our ingredients together, and lends a nice moisture to our products. We use an organic, unsweetened version made by **Santa Cruz** that is free of all allergens.

Arrowroot—Arrowroot is a white starch that comes from the root of the arrowroot (often cassava) plant, found in the tropics. It looks like a fine, white powder, and is another key ingredient in our products at Sweet Freedom. Arrowroot helps to replace eggs, binds ingredients together, and thickens our sauces and ganaches. It is a wonderful alternative to cornstarch, for those who are allergic to corn, and much more digestible to boot! We buy our arrowroot from **Bob's Red Mill**, but there are several companies that produce and/or supply arrowroot that is allergen-free.

Baking Soda—Most bakers would be hard-pressed to survive without baking soda, and we at Sweet Freedom are no different. Luckily, it is one of the few (if only!) ingredients in traditional baking that we do not need to omit. This is because baking soda (sodium bicarbonate) is a naturally occurring product and contains no allergens. There are a million healthy uses for baking soda, but leavening and fluffing our goodies is the priority for us at Sweet Freedom.

Bananas—Bananas are a staple in our pantry at Sweet Freedom. We let them ripen until they are tender and sweet, allowing us to use less of other sweeteners. We puree our bananas in a food processor until they are almost liquid, but a good and thorough hand-mashing would work too.

Berry Jam—You will see some recipes that call for various flavors of jam in this book, and we scoured the market until we found one that suited our needs at Sweet Freedom. **Whole Foods 365 Brand** makes a "Fruit Spread" that is free of sugar, as well as all of the other allergens that we avoid. You can vary the type and flavor of the jam as desired, depending on the recipe, though our favorite flavor is a mixture of different wild berries. If you are so inclined and have the time, making your own jam at home with fresh, organic fruit and a vegan pectin is also a great alternative.

Blueberries—During the summertime, you'll see lots of blueberry-flavored treats at Sweet Freedom when the fresh berries are ripe for the pickin'. Year round, we use fresh-frozen, wild blueberries from **Wyman's of Maine**, as they are among the easiest and healthiest varieties. They are also a great way to get Mother Nature's top antioxidant into your diet while eating something truly ooey-gooey.

Bob's Red Mill Gluten-Free All-Purpose Baking Flour—This staple in our pantry is pretty hard to substitute in certain recipes. **Bob's Red Mill** has done a great job of combining just the right amount of certain gluten-free, allergen-free flours into a mixture so that we didn't need to reinvent the wheel. You'll find that some of our recipes call for this flour mixture, and you can now readily find it in many grocery stores.

Brown Rice Flour—Brown rice flour is a nice addition to a gluten-free flour mixture in any recipe. It contains more fiber and minerals than its more refined counterparts. Not all brown rice flours are created equally, however. Many versions are quite gritty or grainy, leaving an undesired texture to our desserts. We found a great option made by a company called **Authentic Foods** and it is called **Superfine Brown Rice Flour**. It is the best! However, if you can't get your hands on this brand, when in doubt, buy the finest, smoothest brown rice flour you can find.

Candy Cane—Nothing says the holidays like candy cane, and we searched until we found a brand or two that were allergen-free and free of any artificial food dyes. You can find them at **www.naturalcandystore.com**, one of our favorite resources for occasional toppings and garnishes for special events and holidays. You'll find crushed candy cane on top of our Mint Double Chocolate Chip Cupcakes and our Magic Bars, among others, during the holiday season.

Carrots—Freshly shredded carrots make their debut in our Carrot Cake recipe, as well as our Carrot Loaf. We try to use organic carrots whenever possible, and while many first peel the carrots before shredding them, we often leave the outer layer of the carrot on, as that is where much of the nutrients are found. One little word of caution if you do this as well: sometimes organic carrots, when left unpeeled, will turn a slightly greenish hue when they react with the baking soda in a recipe. We prefer to keep the nutrients intact if possible, but if a little green speck here and there just won't work for you, go ahead and peel the carrots before shredding them. Because we often need so many cups of carrots at a time at our commercial bakery, we use the shredding blade on our food processor, but for at-home use, using a hand-held grater with the larger holes will do just fine.

Cayenne Pepper—This spicy powder sneaks into a few of our recipes to give a little kick when we feel like it. Cayenne mixes well with cocoa and also lime for a little Mexican zest here and there. You'll find us using this warming spice during certain holidays for an extra flavor (and metabolism!) boost.

Chocolate Chips—Finding a chocolate chip that met all of our criteria at Sweet Freedom wasn't easy, but we finally settled on **Enjoy Life** brand. Their dark chocolate chips (semisweet) are free of dairy, gluten, and soy, and taste amazing. We use the mini-version in-house, but they sell larger chunks too. The chips do contain evaporated cane juice, so if you're supersensitive to that form of sugar, just tread lightly. **Enjoy Life** chocolate chips are found in many of our recipes, and are also the basis for our ganache—they definitely make our life more enjoyable!

Cinnamon—We love our cinnamon at Sweet Freedom, and you'll see it appear in many of our recipes. Cinnamon is a wonderful, natural blood sugar stabilizer and has a nice warming effect on your system, especially in winter months. During the fall and winter you'll see lots of goodies containing this spice in our display cases and being shipped out daily!

Cloves—Ground cloves appear in many of our recipes around the holidays, and in the fall where we pair this spice with organic pumpkin puree. Cloves have a strong flavor so remember that a little bit goes a long way!

Cocoa Powder—We wouldn't be able to call ourselves a bakery of any sort if we didn't use a ton of cocoa powder! Chocolate lovers will rejoice at all of our recipes that include this vital ingredient. For our purposes at Sweet Freedom, only the best will do. We don't use just any cocoa powder, and we recommend that you invest in a good, quality cocoa too, as the richness and depth of the flavor will shine through. Our favorite cocoa that we buy in bulk comes from the brand, **Bergenfield**. It is a rich mahogany color, is unsweetened, and allergen-free (of course!), and also Dutch alkalized to avoid any funky chemical reactions. The higher the fat content, the richer your chocolate goodies will turn out. We like a 22–24% fat content for richness and mouth-feel.

Coconut—You'll see many coconut products in our recipes because we find it to be such a great flavor and texture addition to the type of baking that we do. The shredded coconut that we use is always unsweetened and organic to ensure it's as pure as can be. We prefer **Bob's Red Mill** brand, but any will do as long as it's unsweetened. (*Read* **Coconut Oil** *listing on the next page, for allergy information regarding coconut products.*)

Coconut Milk—In most of our recipes we use some form of coconut milk. We prefer it to rice milk or other non-dairy alternatives because of the richness in its flavor and healthy fat content. Please be sure to read carefully in each recipe, whether the type of coconut milk called for comes from the carton or can (there is a big difference!). For coconut milk in the carton we use the **So Delicious** unsweetened variety. In the can, the coconut milk should always be full fat, and also organic if possible, as this version tends to have the best outcome, especially for our frosting. The canned coconut milk that we prefer is **Thai Kitchen**, as it is unsweetened, organic, and has no additives. (*Again, see allergy info on the next page under* **Coconut Oil***.*)

Coconut Oil—Ahhh, our beloved coconut oil—what would we do without you? As you'll see, coconut oil appears in just about every Sweet Freedom Bakery recipe, and there are so many reasons why. While coconut oil has previously gotten a bad rap due to its saturated fat content, what we have known for some time and others are beginning to realize, is that saturated fats are not all created equally. The type of saturated fat in coconut oil is a MCT, or medium-chain-triglyceride, meaning that our bodies burn it for energy more quickly, instead of storing it as fat. Coconut oil is also rich in lauric acid, which has antiviral properties to boot. Like butter, coconut oil is a solid at room or cold temperatures, and a liquid at over 72 degrees Fahrenheit. For that reason, our goodies tend to be delicate when left outside at higher temperatures. Please keep that in mind when storing the fruits of your labor, especially anything that involves frosting! Most of our recipes require that the coconut oil used is in liquid (melted) form (but not boiling hot), which we achieve by heating the oil on the stovetop or in the oven for a minute or two prior to baking. You should melt the coconut oil first and then measure the amount you need for each recipe once it's melted. We recommend that you use an expeller-pressed coconut oil to avoid imparting a strong coconut flavor to your recipes. Expeller-pressed coconut oil is neutral in flavor and won't turn rancid when exposed to higher temperatures in the oven. The brand we buy in bulk and recommend is **Tropical Traditions**, but there are many options for finding quality, expeller-pressed coconut oil out there these days.

*Please note that the FDA considers coconut to be a treenut, and if you are allergic to coconut oil, you should use a substitution of your choice. Although not ideal or quite right for our desired texture or flavor, rapeseed and canola are two alternative oil options if you must substitute. We don't recommend any other oil or milk substitute for our Frosting or Whipped Cream, however.

Coconut Sugar—We love coconut sugar! It is our favorite sweetener at Sweet Freedom. We just want to shout it from the mountaintops! When we first opened our doors in 2010, no one had really heard of coconut sugar. Most alternative and allergen-free recipes and bakeries use plain old white sugar because it's easier to bake with and more readily available. We just couldn't live with that. Knowing the detriment of white sugar to our health, we stubbornly developed all of our recipes with coconut sugar wherever possible, even though it was more expensive and gave a slightly tan-ish hue to some of our products. It was worth it to us, because coconut sugar is an unrefined, all-natural sweetener that is very gentle on our blood sugar and won't give you that sugar slump after eating it—much better for our bodies and our mental health too! It comes from the sap of the palm tree, is easily digested, contains minerals and nutrients, and has a wonderful caramel-like flavor not dissimilar to a brown or raw sugar. Coconut sugar has become more readily available at health food stores and online, so be sure to check out our **Approved Sweet Freedom Bakery Suppliers** list *(see page 136)*, on suggestions of where to find it. Sometimes it is also referred to as coconut crystal or palm sugar. If you can't seem to get your hands on any coconut sugar, or you are allergic, raw cane sugar, Florida crystals, or succanat can be decent alternatives to use. In this case you'll have to cut the amount of sugar back by about 25% (so use ¾ of a cup for every 1 cup), as these sugar varieties are sweeter and more potent.

Cranberries—Cranberries are a wonderful flavor and color addition to our recipes, especially in the fall and wintertime. We typically use an organic frozen variety for ease and longevity, but fresh cranberries, when in season, are always a treat! Just remember that the size and water content of any fruit can vary, thus changing the recipe slightly, so be sure and follow the measurement amount that we recommend in each recipe as closely as possible.

Cream of Tartar—Cream of tartar is our favorite substitute to baking powder, as baking powder is corn-derived, and won't do for our allergen-free purposes and delicate recipes. Cream of tartar comes from tartaric acid, a naturally occurring substance in grapes and other tart fruits often used in the winemaking process. It helps to leaven our recipes and lends a nice fluffy texture. You can typically find it in the spice aisle.

Extracts—All of our flavor extracts come from a very special place called **Silver Cloud Estates**. We buy them in bulk and use them generously, because we know that they are free of all allergens and preservatives. They are the purest of the pure, coming straight from the plant source. There are other brands out there now that meet our allergen requirements too, so just be sure to read labels well when shopping in your baking aisle.

Flax Meal—Flax meal (aka ground flax) is not only a great alternative to eggs in a recipe (they form a sticky "goop" when mixed with water), but they provide an extra dose of omega-3 fatty acids and fiber too. You can find flax meal almost anywhere these days, or get whole seeds and grind them in a coffee grinder. Just be sure they are free of your allergens, and stored in the fridge to avoid the oily content of them going rancid.

Fleur de Sel—This chunky and flavorful French sea salt is *sooo* wonderful paired with anything with a caramel flavor. You'll see us sprinkle it as a garnish on our Salted Caramel Cupcakes, as it just adds that certain something. If you don't have any on hand, a larger, granulated sea salt or Himalayan Crystal Salt will do just fine.

Food Coloring—When it comes to food coloring, at Sweet Freedom we choose to avoid anything artificial or synthetic. Most food coloring on the market is chock-full of neurotoxins and chemicals, so we only use a plant-based, all-natural coloring that is safest for everyone, especially those with food sensitivities. Keep in mind that plant-based dyes tend to be more subtle in color than the synthetic variety. There are a few brands out there that make food coloring that is plant-derived, for example, extracted from berries. At Sweet Freedom we use **Seelect Tea** brand, although there are a few other allergen-free brands out there so you have options when choosing the right one for you.

Garbanzo-Fava Bean Flour—Garbanzo-fava bean flour is a wonderful product that comes from milling a mixture of garbanzo beans (chickpeas) and fava beans. It is a great gluten-free flour that adds protein and fiber to our recipes, and pairs especially well with other gluten-free grains. We use **Bob's Red Mill** brand, and there is also a growing list of companies that now make this flour mixture as the demand for it and other gluten-free and grain-free flours increases.

Ginger—Dry, powdered ginger makes an appearance in a few of our recipes, and it is a great warming spice, especially when baking treats during the colder months!

Juices—Orange, lemon, lime, and other juices used in our recipes are typically fresh-squeezed with a small

Juices—Orange, lemon, lime, and other juices used in our recipes are typically fresh-squeezed with a small hand-held citrus juicer, but do whatever works best for you. Just make sure the juice you choose is free of sugar, allergens, and preservatives for best results.

Maple Syrup—Pure maple syrup has a rich, unique flavor, and we love to use this natural sweetener in some of our recipes. To find a good, quality maple syrup, make sure it says "pure" on the label, and not "maple flavored syrup." The pure version is collected from the sap of the tree, and is boiled down to obtain a syrup without chemical agents or preservatives. Pure maple syrup contains minerals such as manganese, iron, zinc, potassium, and trace amounts of vitamins too. How wonderful it is to get your daily dose while indulging in something delicious!

Nutmeg—Ground nutmeg is a wonderful addition to some of our recipes, and it pairs so well with cinnamon. Just be sure to only use the recommended amount, as a little bit goes a long way!

Oats—The co-mingled way that oats and wheat are generally grown and processed these days poses a risk for cross-contamination of allergens. Oats, as a result, often contain gluten. At Sweet Freedom we use only oats that are certified gluten-free. **Bob's Red Mill** makes them, and there are other brands that are safe for those who can generally tolerate gluten-free oats as well.

Potato Starch—Potato starch is a gluten-free addition to some of our flour mixtures that helps keep our goodies light and fluffy instead of dense. We buy our potato starch from **Bob's Red Mill**, though there are many companies that make potato starch that is free of allergens. Make sure you are using potato *starch* and not potato *flour*—there is a difference!

Pumpkin—The fall and winter months wouldn't be the same without yummy pumpkin-filled goodies! Pumpkin is one of our favorite ingredients, especially during that time of year. Canned, unsweetened, organic pumpkin is what we use in most of our recipes, but if you have time to prepare fresh pumpkin that would be great too!

Raisins—Raisins are a great addition to anything with oatmeal! We recommend that you use organic, unsweetened raisins with no added preservatives for the best outcome.

Sea Salt—Sea salt is an important component in our recipes, because it helps to bring out the subtle flavors of our pure ingredients. Salt that naturally comes from the sea is better for your body and your palate than your typical table (ionized) salt that is processed or bleached.

Sorghum Flour—Sorghum is a non-gluten grain that is tan or cream-colored. It comes from a cereal (grassy) grain that is milled to a soft, fine flour. It combines well with other alternative flours to make a well-rounded gluten-free flour mixture. **Bob's Red Mill** is one company that produces sorghum flour, though you'll find there are others out there now as well.

Sweet Rice Flour—Sweet rice flour is another gluten-free option that is used in some of our recipes, and, as its name implies, it imparts a slightly sweeter flavor than traditional rice flours. We like **Authentic Foods** brand because of its super-fine texture, though **Bob's Red Mill** and others make this ingredient too. Sometimes a little sweetness is just needed!

White Rice Flour—White rice flour is a commonly found, gluten-free alternative flour. We like **Authentic Foods** brand and order from them in bulk, but there are many brands who produce white rice flour, so just choose the smoothest, or least grainy version you can find.

Xanthan Gum—Xanthan gum is a plant-based gum that helps to bind our ingredients together, and gives our products a bit of "stretch" or elasticity that is lacking as a result of removing the gluten. Many xanthan gums on the market are corn-derived, so if you're allergic or sensitive to corn, you should be aware of this fact. We buy our xanthan gum from a company called **TIC Gums**, as they remove any corn protein from the xanthan gum.

Zests—The lemon, lime, and orange zests that we recommend in our recipes are freshly grated for purest and freshest flavor. Using a good microplane or citrus zester is your best bet.

Zucchini—Fresh zucchini appears in our Zucchini Loaf and Muffins. We recommend that you freshly grate yours using a large grating box or the grater attachment on a food processor.

TOOLS & KITCHEN GADGETS

What You Will Need

Hand Mixer—We use a hand mixer when making our frosting bases and it is definitely a must! Beyond that you shouldn't need to use a hand mixer much, unless you opt for one in place of where a standing mixer is recommended.

Measuring Cups—This is important! For all of these recipes, you will only use dry measuring cups (the ones that are often metal and have a handle), even for the liquid ingredients. You'll need a set that has $\frac{1}{4}$ cup, $\frac{1}{3}$ cup, $\frac{1}{2}$ cup, and 1 cup.

Measuring Spoons—You will use these in every recipe so make sure you have a durable set! You'll need one that has a $\frac{1}{8}$ teaspoon, $\frac{1}{4}$ teaspoon, $\frac{1}{2}$ teaspoon, 1 teaspoon, $\frac{1}{2}$ tablespoon, and 1 tablespoon.

Parchment Paper—We use a lot of parchment paper at Sweet Freedom. It is a big help and time-saver to line the cookie sheets with it, and we make a lot of batches of fresh cookies each day! A little trick: You can flip each sheet over after the cookies have been removed and use the other side.

Sifter or Mesh Colander—A little Sweet Freedom trick: if the flour or coconut sugar you are using seems to have clumps in it, it helps to sift it through a strainer with small holes into the mixing bowl. Any larger granules that don't go through the holes can either be discarded, or further sifted by taking the back of the measuring cup and pushing down gently to coax the granules to break into smaller pieces.

Spatulas—A sturdy rubber spatula that stands up at high temperatures is always a good kitchen tool. You'll want to get every last bit of batter out of that mixing bowl, so make sure you have a good one to help you! Also, a metal spatula with a thin, flexible (bendy) tip will especially help you after your cookies are cooled and ready to be removed from the cookie sheet.

Scoops—We use various sizes of ice cream scoops to fill our cupcake liners and muffin liners (never more than $\frac{3}{4}$ of the way full!), to scoop cookie batter onto cookie sheets, or to add frosting to our cookie sandwiches. Melon ballers are also nice tools to use when you want a mini-sized cookie.

Stand Mixer—A stand mixer is a helpful kitchen appliance if you can invest in one. You will find it handy for finishing our frostings, Magic Bars, and pie crusts, to name a few. Not to worry if you don't have a stand mixer, though—a hand mixer will do the trick too.

Whisk—A great wire whisk goes a long way when mixing our dry and wet ingredients separately. If the batter gets too thick once you combine the wet and dry together, you can always switch to a rubber spatula or wooden spoon where warranted.

Citrus Juicer—A small hand-held juicer is a handy gadget for squeezing out that fresh juice when called for in our recipes.

Cupcake Corer or Paring Knife—A few of our cupcakes involve a creamy, gooey filling. The best way to fill them is to either use a cupcake corer (yes, they make these!), or simply cut a cylindrical cone shape out of the middle of the cupcake with a sharp paring knife (only go about halfway to the bottom of the cupcake). Fill the resulting space with plenty of yummy goodness.

Grater, Microplane, Zester, Food Processor—Any of these tools will do when grating or zesting our ingredients is required. Choose whichever one works best for you!

Frosting Bag & Tips, Frosting Spatula—These are important tools to use when frosting our cupcakes. Choose whatever size tip and bag with which you're most comfortable, and remember that when piping or applying frosting, practice makes perfect!

Double Boiler—A double boiler is a great tool to use when melting delicate cocoa products, such as chocolate chips. If you don't have a double boiler, you can also boil a pot of water and place a medium metal mixing bowl containing the chocolate over the top of the boiling water and stir until the chocolate chips are melted. Either method will help you avoid burning the chocolate.

Squeeze Bottles—A few plastic squeeze bottles will come in handy when decorating or glazing our desserts. Fill them with the appropriate glaze or sauce and squeeze away!

Pans and Tins—Cake pans (8″ round), cookie sheets, cruller pans, cupcake/muffin tins, doughnut pans, loaf pans (standard size 5″ x 10″ and mini-sized), pie pan (9″ round), and medium saucepans will all be helpful to have on hand. Make sure you invest in pans and tins that have a solid, sturdy metal bottom for best results.

Other gadgets—You will want to have on hand mixing bowls (small and medium), a cutting board, oven mitts, cake testers or toothpicks, cookie cutters, cooling racks, an oven thermometer (make sure your oven is calibrated correctly), and a good timer.

OTHER IMPORTANT TIPS

Storing your Sweet Freedom Treats

This is very crucial! The key to keeping your Sweet Freedom treats fresh and moist is to store them at room temperature (not near a heat source), and wrap or cover them so that they are airtight. We recommend you keep them on your kitchen counter in a cookie tin, a Tupperware container, or wrapped tightly in plastic wrap to avoid air getting in and drying your goodies out. This way, they should stay fresh for several days.

Heat Sensitivity

We mentioned this before, but because most of these recipes contain coconut oil, which turns to a liquid at temperatures above 72 degrees, you don't want to put these desserts in a hot area. If you're bringing them somewhere during warmer weather, transport them quickly, or in a cooler. Don't leave them in your car, or out in the sun! On the flip-side, you also don't want to store most of your Sweet Freedom baked goods for long periods in the refrigerator, as we find it tends to dry them out. Again, Sweet Freedom treats are in their "happy place" when wrapped airtight at room temperature.

What to Refrigerate—the Exceptions to the Rule

The refrigerator is a good place to store your frostings and glazes. We keep all of our frostings in airtight containers in the refrigerator (if there is any left over!). Also, the fridge is a good place for other perishable ingredients (such as opened coconut milk cartons or applesauce, ground flax, certain produce, jams, and juices).

Freezing Your Goodies for the Long Haul

You can pretty much freeze any of these desserts so that you can tap into them for months to come. We find that just about all of them keep well when frozen for several weeks and sometimes months. Just be sure that they are in some sort of airtight container before you pop them into the freezer or they will dry out!

Substituting Ingredients

While there are various substitutes in the allergen-free baking world (depending on what your specific allergies and intolerances are), wherever possible, we recommend that you don't substitute our recommended ingredients if you can avoid it at all! We just can't vouch for the outcome.

COOKIES, BARS, AND SQUARES

CHOCOLATE CHIP COOKIES
Yields 24 cookies

This was the very first recipe that I developed when the plans for opening Sweet Freedom were underway. I had experimented with a few different versions before landing on this one. I would make a cookie batter and bake one cookie at a time, let my husband Jon try it, and change the batter as needed until I got it right. I think that the secret ingredient was the coconut sugar. It really makes the recipe, as it has a brown-sugar-like taste that just brings me back to those sinful (allergen-filled) cookies of my childhood. If you're a spoon-licker like me, just note that this is one of the few recipes in this book whose raw batter doesn't taste as good as the baked version. But after just eleven minutes of baking, eaten warm right out of the oven, these cookies hit the spot!

Ingredients

STEP ONE (dry ingredients)
2 cups Bob's Red Mill gluten-free all-purpose baking flour*
1½ cups coconut sugar
¼ cup flax meal
1½ teaspoons xanthan gum
1 teaspoon baking soda

Note: For Double Chocolate Chip and Mint Double Chocolate Chip Cookies reduce Bob's gluten-free all-purpose baking flour to 1½ cups and add ½ cup cocoa powder

STEP TWO (wet ingredients)
1 cup melted coconut oil
6 tablespoons unsweetened applesauce
2 tablespoons vanilla extract
1 teaspoon sea salt

STEP THREE
1 cup dark chocolate chips

Note: For Mint Double Chocolate Chip Cookies add 2 teaspoons peppermint extract.

Instructions

Preheat the oven to 350°F. Line a sheet pan or cookie sheet with parchment paper.

STEP ONE
In a medium bowl, sift the dry ingredients and mix them together.

STEP TWO
In a large bowl, mix together the wet ingredients. Then add the dry mixture to the wet mixture and stir them until a grainy dough is formed.

STEP THREE
Gently fold the chocolate chips into the dough until they are evenly distributed. Using an ice cream scoop or similar tool, scoop the dough onto the prepared baking sheets about an inch apart. Flatten the cookies slightly with the back of the scoop. (Note: If the dough seems too oily or spreads too thin on the cookie sheet, additional Bob's gluten-free all-purpose baking flour may be sprinkled into the dough until desired consistency is achieved, up to ½ cup).

STEP FOUR
Bake the cookies for 9 minutes. Rotate the sheet and bake for 2 additional minutes. Let cool completely.

*A great option for these or any of the cookies is to create **Cookie Sandwiches** using 2 tablespoons of frosting between 2 cookies of your choice. Suggested as a filling is **Vanilla Frosting** (see recipe on page 76).*

CHOCOLATE CHIP BLONDIES

Yields 12 mini loaves, or one 9" x 13" pan

Blondies are such a fun, vanilla-flavored alternative to the brownie. They can be baked in any format that you like—a brownie pan, small or large cupcake/muffin pan, etc. At the bakery, we often recommend these to customers who call and want mini treats for their small child's birthday. Add a dollop of frosting on top, and they are definitely a kid-pleaser.

Ingredients

STEP ONE (dry ingredients)
1½ cups coconut sugar
½ cup garbanzo-fava bean flour
½ cup brown rice flour (superfine)
½ cup potato starch
¼ cup arrowroot
1 teaspoon cream of tartar
1 teaspoon sea salt
1 teaspoon xanthan gum
¾ teaspoon baking soda

STEP TWO (wet ingredients)
½ cup melted coconut oil
½ cup hot water
⅓ cup unsweetened applesauce
2 tablespoons vanilla extract

STEP THREE
1 cup dark chocolate chips

Instructions

Preheat the oven to 350°F. Lightly oil with coconut oil twelve 2" x 4" mini loaf pans or one 9" x 13" baking pan.

STEP ONE
In a medium bowl, sift the dry ingredients and mix them together.

STEP TWO
In a large bowl, mix together the wet ingredients. Then add the dry mixture to the wet mixture, stirring with a spatula until well-combined.

STEP THREE
Gently fold the chocolate chips into the batter until they are evenly distributed. Fill the pan(s) about ¾ of the way full with the batter.

STEP FOUR
For mini loaves: Bake for 7 minutes. Rotate and bake for 7 more minutes.

For 9" x 13" pan: Bake for 20 minutes. Rotate and bake for an additional 10 minutes. (This size will yield roughly 20 to 30 squares, depending on your cut size).

Let them cool for 10 minutes before removing from loaf pans or baking pan.

CHOCOLATE DIPPED MACAROONS

Yields 14 cookies

For those who love coconut, these macaroons are the perfect little bite-sized treat. With only a few ingredients and steps, this was one of the simplest recipes to develop, and it is a good one to start out with if you're a little gun-shy with baking. I like to dip them in chocolate ganache, because to me, no dessert is complete without a little dark chocolate!

Ingredients

STEP ONE (macaroon ingredients)
$2^1/_3$ cups unsweetened shredded coconut
$^2/_3$ cup coconut milk, canned
$^1/_3$ cup brown rice flour (superfine)
$^1/_3$ cup agave nectar
1 teaspoon vanilla extract
$^1/_4$ teaspoon cream of tartar
$^1/_4$ teaspoon baking soda

STEP FOUR
Chocolate Ganache *(see recipe on page 83)*

Instructions

Preheat the oven to 375°F. Line a large cookie sheet with parchment paper.

STEP ONE
In a medium bowl, combine the ingredients for the macaroons, mixing them well. Set the bowl aside for about 5 minutes to allow the coconut to absorb the liquid.

Note: You should have a thick batter, but it will not be very cohesive.

STEP TWO
Using an ice cream scoop or similar tool, firmly pack the dough into the scoop. Drop the batter onto the cookie sheet, forming it into egg-shaped mounds about an inch in length. Using the back of the scoop, make an indent in the middle of each mound.

STEP THREE
Bake the macaroons for 8 minutes. Rotate and bake for 6 more minutes or until the coconut begins to brown. Remove them from the oven, and place them into the refrigerator to harden.

STEP FOUR
Dip each macaroon halfway into the chocolate ganache to coat. Return the dipped macaroons to the refrigerator for about 20 minutes to harden the ganache.

CHOCOLATE CAYENNE LIME COOKIE CAKE

Yields one 8" cookie cake

At Sweet Freedom, we can take any of our cookie recipes and make them into a cookie cake. A cookie cake is an easy alternative to a traditional cake, and by decorating it with frosting at the end you're not missing a thing! This variation has a nice combination of rich chocolate, a tang of lime, and a nice little kick to your taste buds at the end.

Ingredients

STEP ONE (dry ingredients)
1 ½ cups Bob's Red Mill gluten-free
   all-purpose baking flour
1 ½ cups coconut sugar
½ cup cocoa powder
¼ cup flax meal
1 ½ teaspoons xanthan gum
1 teaspoon baking soda
1 teaspoon sea salt
½ teaspoon cayenne pepper

STEP TWO (wet ingredients)
1 cup melted coconut oil
6 tablespoons unsweetened applesauce
1 ½ teaspoons vanilla extract
1 ½ teaspoons lime zest
½ teaspoon lime extract

STEP THREE
1 cup dark chocolate chips

STEP FIVE
Vanilla Frosting *(see recipe on page 76)**
Zest of 1 to 2 limes (optional)

*Note: The frosting recipe takes at least 6 hours to prepare, including freezing and refrigeration time. Plan accordingly.

Instructions

Preheat the oven to 350°F. Grease an 8-inch round cake pan with coconut oil, and then line with parchment paper.

STEP ONE
In a medium bowl, sift the dry ingredients and mix them together.

STEP TWO
In a large bowl, mix together the wet ingredients. Using a rubber spatula, carefully add the dry mixture to the wet mixture and stir them until a grainy dough is formed.

STEP THREE
Gently fold in the chocolate chips until they are evenly distributed throughout the dough. Pour the prepared dough into the baking pan.

STEP FOUR
Bake the cookie cake for 33 minutes. Let it cool completely.

STEP FIVE
Decorate the cake with the prepared frosting. Garnish with lime zest (optional).

OATMEAL RAISIN COOKIES

Yields 27 cookies

In my opinion, no dessert cookbook would be complete without an oatmeal raisin cookie recipe. These cookies are such a classic treat. When I was developing this recipe I knew I was on to something once I had added in the maple syrup, because it just gave the cookies that extra layer of flavor. In our house there is nothing wrong with eating these cookies for breakfast! At Sweet Freedom, the oatmeal raisin cookie sandwich is one of our best sellers. With a thick layer of vanilla frosting in the middle, what's there not to love?

Ingredients

STEP ONE (dry ingredients)
2 cups Bob's Red Mill gluten-free
    all-purpose baking flour
1¼ cups coconut sugar
¼ cup flax meal
1½ teaspoons xanthan gum
1 teaspoon baking soda
1 teaspoon cinnamon
1 teaspoon sea salt
¼ teaspoon nutmeg

STEP TWO (wet ingredients)
1 cup + 6 tablespoons melted coconut oil
½ cup unsweetened applesauce
¼ cup maple syrup
2 tablespoons vanilla extract

STEP THREE
1¼ cups oats
1 cup raisins

Instructions

Preheat the oven to 350°F. Line a cookie sheet with parchment paper.

STEP ONE
In a medium bowl, sift the dry ingredients and mix them together.

STEP TWO
In a large bowl, mix together the wet ingredients. Add the dry mixture to the wet mixture and stir them until a grainy dough is formed.

STEP THREE
Gently fold in the oats and raisins until they are evenly distributed throughout the dough. Using an ice cream scoop or similar tool, scoop the batter onto the prepared baking sheet, about an inch apart. Flatten the cookies slightly with the back of the scoop.

FYI: It can be helpful to dip the scoop occasionally in water to avoid the cookie dough sticking to the scoop.

STEP FOUR
Bake the cookies for 9 minutes. Rotate and bake them for 3 additional minutes.

Note: The finished cookies will be slightly crispy on the outside and soft in the center.

RASPBERRY LEMON BARS

Yields 35 bars

These Raspberry Lemon Bars make a great summertime dessert if you like fruit-flavored treats. The subtle tang of the lemon and the sweetness of the raspberry are the perfect combination. For a really decadent treat, eat it warm with a dollop of **Ryan's "Whipped Cream"** *(see recipe on page 80)* and maybe even a little extra raspberry filling drizzled on top. Because this recipe yields a lot of bars, this is a good one to freeze any leftovers (wrapped airtight) for later. In my house, however, leftovers don't exist!

Ingredients

STEP ONE (wet ingredients)
1 cup coconut oil, solid
1½ cups coconut sugar
½ cup unsweetened applesauce
2 tablespoons vanilla extract

STEP TWO (dry ingredients)
3½ cups Bob's Red Mill gluten-free all-purpose baking flour
1 teaspoon baking soda
1 teaspoon cream of tartar
1 teaspoon xanthan gum
½ teaspoon sea salt

STEP THREE (raspberry filling)
1½ cups raspberries, thawed or fresh
1 10-oz. jar unsweetened raspberry jam
¼ cup coconut sugar
½ cup arrowroot
¼ cup water

STEP FOUR (crumb topping)
1½ cups oats
1¼ cups brown rice flour (superfine)
¾ cup coconut sugar
½ cup melted coconut oil
¾ teaspoon sea salt

STEP FIVE
Lemon Glaze *(see recipe on page 83)*

Instructions

Preheat the oven to 350°F. Lightly grease a rimmed 12" x 17" (or similar size) cookie sheet or baking pan with coconut oil, and then line the bottom with parchment paper.

STEP ONE
In a large bowl of a standing mixer on medium speed, (or with a hand mixer) mix together the solid coconut oil and coconut sugar. Then add in the applesauce and vanilla extract.

STEP TWO
In a separate bowl, sift together the dry ingredients. Add them to the wet mixture and continue to mix (if using mixer, set on medium speed) until well-combined. Spread the batter onto the sheet pan. Bake the crust for 20 minutes and let cool.

STEP THREE
In a medium saucepan, cook the raspberries, raspberry jam, and coconut sugar over medium heat until the berries are broken down. Meanwhile, mix the arrowroot with water in a small bowl to form a smooth paste. Slowly stir the arrowroot paste into the berry mixture and heat at medium high until a gentle boil begins. Stir the mixture constantly until it thickens to a gel-like consistency. Remove the mixture from the heat and set it aside to cool. Spread the cooled berry filling evenly over the crust.

STEP FOUR
In a medium bowl, mix together the crumb topping ingredients. Evenly cover the berry filling with the crumb mixture. Bake for 25 minutes and let it cool (about 20 minutes). Transfer the bars into the refrigerator to chill fully. Cut the bars into 2½" x 2½" squares.

STEP FIVE
Garnish bars with the Lemon Glaze.

MAGIC BARS
Yields 18 bars

My best friend, Sheryl, and I developed this recipe together one night in my kitchen. She was visiting me from New York for the weekend, and we had just finished dinner. The dessert craving was strong and I was under the gun to add more recipes to the bakery's menu before we opened a few weeks later. I came up with the crust first, and was just going to eat it as a yummy cookie on its own, but I felt that it needed a little something else. Dark chocolate and coconut layered on top were the perfect answer! Now, this is one of my favorite treats at Sweet Freedom, not only because it tastes so yummy, but because every bite reminds me of Sheryl too!

Ingredients

STEP ONE (dry ingredients)
2 cups brown rice flour (superfine)
¼ cup + 2 tablespoons coconut sugar
¼ teaspoon + ⅛ teaspoon sea salt

STEP TWO (wet ingredients)
¾ cup melted coconut oil
¾ cup maple syrup
1½ tablespoons vanilla extract

STEP FOUR (topping)
1½ cups dark chocolate chips
1½ tablespoons melted coconut oil
½ cup unsweetened shredded coconut

Instructions

Preheat the oven to 375°F. Lightly grease an 8" x 8" pan with coconut oil.

STEP ONE
In a medium bowl, sift the dry ingredients and mix them together.

STEP TWO
In a large bowl of a standing mixer, combine the wet ingredients, stirring until well-mixed. Very slowly add in the dry mixture a little at a time. Continue until all of the dry mixture is incorporated.

STEP THREE
Spread the batter evenly into the baking pan. Bake the crust for 18 minutes. Let it cool for 5 minutes.

STEP FOUR
Combine the chocolate chips and coconut oil in a double boiler until they are melted and smooth. Spread the chocolate mixture evenly over the crust and sprinkle the shredded coconut on top. Place the Magic Bars in the refrigerator to harden the chocolate. After the chocolate hardens, remove them from the refrigerator and bring them to room temperature. Cut them into 2" x 2" bars.

CUPCAKES

VANILLA CUPCAKES
Yields 20 cupcakes

Ahhh, the vanilla cupcake—a classic all-American dessert. With its pure vanilla flavor it seems so simple to create. But all was not what it would seem when I was trying to come up with an allergen-free version of this recipe! The vanilla cupcake was the hardest recipe of all to develop, exactly *because* it has such a pure vanilla flavor. The coconut sugar that I was using kept giving the cake a brownish hue, and the texture wasn't quite right at first. Eventually, after many trashed batches, I landed on just the right combo of ingredients. And I'm so grateful that I did, because it led me to be able to expand upon them and morph this recipe into so many other cupcake flavors and varieties, which you will get to enjoy in this chapter. Once you get the vanilla down, the sky's the limit!

Ingredients

STEP ONE (wet ingredients)
½ cup coconut milk (carton)
2 teaspoons apple cider vinegar

STEP TWO (dry ingredients)
1¼ cups coconut sugar
1 cup sorghum flour
1 cup potato starch
1 cup white rice flour
½ cup arrowroot
1 tablespoon cream of tartar
1 teaspoon baking soda
1 teaspoon sea salt
½ teaspoon xanthan gum

STEP THREE (wet ingredients)
1 cup hot water
½ cup melted coconut oil
½ cup agave nectar
3 tablespoons vanilla extract

STEP SIX
Vanilla or Chocolate Frosting *(see recipes on pages 76 and 79)**

*Note: The frosting recipe takes at least 6 hours to prepare, including freezing and refrigeration time. Plan accordingly.

Instructions

Preheat the oven to 350°F. Line muffin tins with paper liners.

STEP ONE
In a medium bowl, mix together the coconut milk and the apple cider vinegar and set aside for 5 minutes.

STEP TWO
In a separate medium bowl, sift the dry ingredients and mix them together.

STEP THREE
Add the remaining wet ingredients into the coconut milk/apple cider mixture.

STEP FOUR
Slowly add the dry mixture into the wet mixture and whisk them until smooth. Fill each paper cupcake liner ¾ of the way full with batter.

STEP FIVE
Bake for 15 minutes. Rotate and bake for 3 more minutes. Let the cupcakes cool for 20 minutes before removing them from the pan.

STEP SIX
Once the cupcakes have completely cooled to room temperature, frost them with the prepared frosting.

BERRY DELIGHT CUPCAKES
Yields 20 cupcakes

This recipe is essentially the vanilla cupcake recipe with an added, fruity twist. Filling each cupcake with berry jam (any berry flavor that you choose will be delish!) and adding some berry frosting on top makes it a delicious treat for those who love a little fruit with their dessert. Just be sure to use a berry jam that doesn't contain a lot of extra sugars and fillers. The cupcake and frosting itself are sweet enough!

Ingredients

STEP ONE (wet ingredients)
½ cup coconut milk (carton)
2 teaspoons apple cider vinegar

STEP TWO (dry ingredients)
1¼ cups coconut sugar
1 cup sorghum flour
1 cup potato starch
1 cup white rice flour
½ cup arrowroot
1 tablespoon cream of tartar
1 teaspoon baking soda
1 teaspoon sea salt
½ teaspoon xanthan gum

STEP THREE (wet ingredients)
1 cup hot water
½ cup melted coconut oil
½ cup agave nectar
3 tablespoons vanilla extract

STEP SIX
1 10-oz. jar unsweetened berry jam
Berry Frosting *(see recipe on page 79)**
Fresh fruit (optional)
Unsweetened jam (optional)

*Note: The frosting recipe takes at least 6 hours to prepare, including freezing and refrigeration time. Plan accordingly.

Instructions

Preheat the oven to 350°F. Line muffin tins with paper liners.

STEP ONE
In a medium bowl, mix together the coconut milk and the apple cider vinegar and set aside for 5 minutes.

STEP TWO
In a separate medium bowl, sift the dry ingredients and mix them together.

STEP THREE
Add the remaining wet ingredients into the coconut milk/apple cider mixture.

STEP FOUR
Slowly add the dry mixture into the wet mixture and whisk until smooth. Fill each paper cupcake liner ¾ of the way full with batter.

STEP FIVE
Bake for 15 minutes. Rotate and bake for 3 more minutes. Let the cupcakes cool for 20 minutes before removing them from the pan.

STEP SIX
Once the cupcakes have completely cooled to room temperature, hollow out each cupcake *(see **Cupcake Corer or Paring Knife** on page 22 for instructions on this process)*. Fill each cupcake with unsweetened berry jam of your choice. Then frost the cupcakes with the prepared frosting. Garnish with fresh fruit and a dollop of jam (optional).

COCONUT LIME CUPCAKES

Yields 20 cupcakes

This recipe is a wonderful and refreshing summertime treat. The lime zest and the creamy vanilla flavor make for a really great combo. You can substitute fresh-squeezed lime juice for lime extract and the flavor will be just as great. These cupcakes remind me of an island vacation in St. Thomas where our family has a house. Topping the cupcake with a cocktail umbrella makes me feel like I'm really there!

Ingredients

STEP ONE (wet ingredients)
½ cup coconut milk (carton)
2 teaspoons apple cider vinegar

STEP TWO (dry ingredients)
1¼ cups coconut sugar
1 cup sorghum flour
1 cup potato starch
1 cup white rice flour
¼ cup arrowroot
1 tablespoon cream of tartar
1 teaspoon baking soda
1 teaspoon sea salt
½ teaspoon xanthan gum

STEP THREE (wet ingredients)
1½ cups shredded coconut
1 cup hot water
¾ cup melted coconut oil
½ cup agave nectar
1 tablespoon + 2 teaspoons lime extract
1 tablespoon + 1 teaspoon lime zest
1 tablespoon + ½ teaspoon vanilla extract
1 tablespoon + ½ teaspoon coconut extract

STEP SIX
Coconut Lime Cream Frosting *(see recipe on page 79)**
Zest of 1 to 2 limes (optional)
20 cocktail umbrellas (optional)

*Note: The frosting recipe takes at least 6 hours to prepare, including freezing and refrigeration time. Plan accordingly.

Instructions

Preheat the oven to 350°F. Line muffin tins with paper liners.

STEP ONE
In a medium bowl, mix together the coconut milk and the apple cider vinegar and set aside for 5 minutes.

STEP TWO
In a separate medium bowl, sift the dry ingredients and mix them together.

STEP THREE
Add the remaining wet ingredients into the coconut milk/apple cider mixture.

STEP FOUR
Slowly add the dry mixture into the wet mixture and whisk until smooth. Fill each paper cupcake liner ¾ of the way full with batter.

STEP FIVE
Bake for 15 minutes. Rotate and bake for 5 more minutes. Let the cupcakes cool for 20 minutes before removing them from the pan.

STEP SIX
Once the cupcakes have fully cooled to room temperature, frost them with the prepared frosting. Garnish them with the lime zest and cocktail umbrellas (optional).

LEMON CUPCAKES
Yields 20 cupcakes

I have found that people either love lemon-flavored desserts, or they *really* don't care for them. I was shocked, however, to be able to convert so many non-lemon-lovers with this simple lemon cupcake recipe. I think the secret is hidden in the fact that we don't use any artificial flavoring or extracts to achieve that fresh lemon flavor. We use only fresh lemon juice, natural extracts, and zest in our recipes, and paired with the vanilla here, it is a definite crowd pleaser. Dust off that zester or microplane and share this recipe with others. They won't even know that the fresh lemon is actually helping to balance their body's natural pH, and make them more alkaline and equipped to fight disease. Who says dessert has to be bad for you?

Ingredients

STEP ONE (wet ingredients)
½ cup coconut milk (carton)
2 teaspoons apple cider vinegar

STEP TWO (dry ingredients)
1¼ cups coconut sugar
1 cup sorghum flour
1 cup potato starch
1 cup white rice flour
½ cup arrowroot
1 tablespoon cream of tartar
1 teaspoon baking soda
1 teaspoon sea salt
½ teaspoon xanthan gum

STEP THREE (wet ingredients)
1 cup hot water
½ cup melted coconut oil
½ cup agave nectar
2 tablespoons + 1 teaspoon vanilla
    extract
1 tablespoon + 2 teaspoons lemon extract
1 tablespoon + 1 teaspoon lemon zest

STEP SIX
Lemon Cream Frosting *(see recipe on
    page 79)*
Zest of 1 lemon (optional)

*Note: The frosting recipe takes at least
6 hours to prepare, including freezing
and refrigeration time. Plan accordingly.*

Instructions

Preheat the oven to 350°F. Line muffin tins with paper liners.

STEP ONE
In a medium bowl, mix together the coconut milk and the apple cider vinegar and set aside for 5 minutes.

STEP TWO
In a separate medium bowl, sift the dry ingredients and mix them together.

STEP THREE
Add the remaining wet ingredients into the coconut milk/apple cider mixture.

STEP FOUR
Slowly add the dry mixture into the wet mixture and whisk until smooth. Fill each paper cupcake liner ¾ of the way full with batter.

STEP FIVE
Bake for 15 minutes. Rotate and bake for 3 more minutes. Let the cupcakes cool for 20 minutes before removing them from the pan.

STEP SIX
Once the cupcakes have completely cooled to room temperature, frost them with the prepared frosting. Garnish with lemon zest (optional).

ORANGE CREAMSICLE CUPCAKES

Yields 20 cupcakes

Who doesn't think of their childhood when tasting anything flavored like an orange creamsicle? It makes me think of summers at the beach and hearing with excitement the melody of the beloved ice cream truck. Unfortunately this treat is usually laden with dairy, white sugar, and a host of artificial ingredients that will wreak havoc on your health. I know it did mine! That's why I developed this flavor of cupcake without all of the allergens and chemicals that usually come with it. I'm so excited to be able to give this yummy recipe and positive memory to my little ones without all of the side effects that come with it.

Ingredients

STEP ONE (wet ingredients)
½ cup coconut milk (carton)
2 teaspoons apple cider vinegar

STEP TWO (dry ingredients)
1 ¼ cups coconut sugar
1 cup sorghum flour
1 cup potato starch
1 cup white rice flour
½ cup arrowroot
1 tablespoon cream of tartar
1 teaspoon baking soda
1 teaspoon sea salt
½ teaspoon xanthan gum

STEP THREE (wet ingredients)
1 cup hot water
½ cup melted coconut oil
½ cup agave nectar
2 tablespoons + 2 teaspoons orange juice
1 tablespoon + 1 teaspoon vanilla extract
1 tablespoon + 1 teaspoon orange zest

STEP SIX
Vanilla Frosting *(see recipe on page 76)**
Zest of 1 orange (optional)
20 popsicle sticks (optional)

Note: The frosting recipe takes at least 6 hours to prepare, including freezing and refrigeration time. Plan accordingly.

Instructions

Preheat the oven to 350°F. Line muffin tins with paper liners.

STEP ONE
In a medium bowl, mix together the coconut milk and the apple cider vinegar and set aside for 5 minutes.

STEP TWO
In a separate medium bowl, sift the dry ingredients and mix them together.

STEP THREE
Add the remaining wet ingredients into the coconut milk/apple cider mixture.

STEP FOUR
Slowly add the dry mixture into the wet mixture and whisk until smooth. Fill each paper cupcake liner ¾ of the way full with batter.

STEP FIVE
Bake for 15 minutes. Rotate and bake for 3 more minutes. Let the cupcakes cool for 20 minutes before removing them from the pan.

STEP SIX
Once the cupcakes have completely cooled to room temperature, frost them with the prepared frosting. Garnish with orange zest and a popsicle stick (optional).

SAMOA CUPCAKES

Yields 20 cupcakes

I'll be the first to admit that the Samoa was my ultimate favorite cookie when I was growing up. I donned my Brownie uniform proudly, probably in part, because I got to sell (and eat!) these tasty cookies. This is why we just had to come up with a cupcake version of this cookie at the bakery. The pairing of dark chocolate, our own vegan caramel, and coconut flakes on top of our classic vanilla cupcake recipe has reinvented this special treat for me. With this healthier, allergen-free version of the cookie, there's no need for the original anymore! My immune system is thankful for that!

Ingredients

STEP ONE (wet ingredients)
½ cup coconut milk (carton)
2 teaspoons apple cider vinegar

STEP TWO (dry ingredients)
1¼ cups coconut sugar
1 cup sorghum flour
1 cup potato starch
1 cup white rice flour
½ cup arrowroot
1 tablespoon cream of tartar
1 teaspoon baking soda
1 teaspoon sea salt
½ teaspoon xanthan gum

STEP THREE (wet ingredients)
1 cup hot water
¾ cup agave nectar
½ cup melted coconut oil
3 tablespoons vanilla extract

STEP SIX
Chocolate Ganache *(see recipe on page 83)*
Caramel Sauce *(see recipe on page 82)*
Vanilla Frosting *(see recipe on page 76)**
½ to 1 cup shredded coconut, lightly toasted**

*Note: The frosting recipe takes at least 6 hours to prepare, including freezing and refrigeration time. Plan accordingly.

**Note: Put a single layer of shredded coconut on a cookie sheet and toast for about 5 minutes at 350°F until the edges are light brown.

Instructions

Preheat the oven to 350°F. Line muffin tins with paper liners.

STEP ONE
In a medium bowl, mix together the coconut milk and the apple cider vinegar and set aside for 5 minutes.

STEP TWO
In a separate medium bowl, sift the dry ingredients and mix them together.

STEP THREE
Add the remaining wet ingredients into the coconut milk/apple cider mixture.

STEP FOUR
Slowly add the dry mixture into the wet mixture and whisk until smooth. Fill each paper cupcake liner ¾ of the way full with batter.

STEP FIVE
Bake for 15 minutes. Rotate and bake for 3 more minutes. Let the cupcakes cool for 20 minutes before removing them from the pan.

STEP SIX
Once the cupcakes have completely cooled to room temperature, hollow out each cupcake *(see **Cupcake Corer or Paring Knife** on page 22 for instructions on this process)*. Fill each cupcake halfway with warm chocolate ganache. Then fill the rest with caramel sauce. Frost the cupcakes with the prepared frosting. Dip the frosted cupcakes in the toasted coconut, covering the tops completely. To top it off, drizzle each cupcake with caramel sauce on top in one direction and chocolate ganache in the other direction.

CHOCOLATE CUPCAKES

Yields 22 cupcakes

This rich dark chocolate cupcake paired with either chocolate, vanilla, or mocha frosting should not be underestimated. I would say that the deep chocolate flavor in this cupcake is more of an "adult" flavor, suited to those with a more sophisticated palate, and to me its sheer perfection (if I do say so!). It's really important with this recipe, even more than others, to use the highest quality cocoa that you can find. At Sweet Freedom we use a cocoa powder that has a higher fat content than most, and the richness in flavor really shines through as a result. There's nothing to feel guilty about here, however. Dark cocoa is a natural antioxidant, and the fattier variety contains more cocoa butter, which increases the number of essential minerals such as iron, magnesium, manganese, and zinc—all of which support your heart, bones, and immune system.

Ingredients

STEP ONE (wet ingredients)
½ cup coconut milk (carton)
2 teaspoons apple cider vinegar

STEP TWO (dry ingredients)
1¼ cups coconut sugar
1 cup sorghum flour
1 cup cocoa powder
½ cup potato starch
½ cup brown rice flour (superfine)
¼ cup arrowroot
1 tablespoon cream of tartar
1 teaspoon baking soda
1 teaspoon sea salt
½ teaspoon xanthan gum

STEP THREE (wet ingredients)
1 cup hot water
¾ cup melted coconut oil
¾ cup agave nectar
1 tablespoon vanilla extract

STEP SIX
Vanilla, Chocolate, or Mocha Frosting *(see recipes on pages 76 and 79)**

*Note: The frosting recipe takes at least 6 hours to prepare, including freezing and refrigeration time. Plan accordingly.

Instructions

Preheat the oven to 350°F. Line muffin tins with paper liners.

STEP ONE
In a medium bowl, mix together the coconut milk and the apple cider vinegar and set aside for 5 minutes.

STEP TWO
In a separate medium bowl, sift the dry ingredients and mix them together.

STEP THREE
Add the remaining wet ingredients into the coconut milk/apple cider mixture.

STEP FOUR
Slowly add the dry mixture into the wet mixture and whisk until smooth. Fill each paper cupcake liner ¾ of the way full with batter.

STEP FIVE
Bake for 15 minutes. Rotate and bake for 3 more minutes. Let the cupcakes cool for 20 minutes before removing them from the pan.

STEP SIX
Once the cupcakes have completely cooled to room temperature, frost them with the prepared frosting of your choice.

MINT DOUBLE CHOCOLATE CHIP CUPCAKES

Yields 22 cupcakes

These rich and minty cupcakes are not for the faint of heart. This is one of my favorite recipes, because it combines two of my favorite flavors—chocolate and mint. When I was pregnant with my son, Chase, I craved these cupcakes like no other! Sometimes I would make some homemade coconut milk vanilla ice cream to go on top. The mint extract that we use at the bakery is as pure as can be—from Silvercloud Estates—and I think it makes all the difference in flavor.

Ingredients

STEP ONE (wet ingredients)
½ cup coconut milk (carton)
2 teaspoons apple cider vinegar

STEP TWO (dry ingredients)
1¼ cups coconut sugar
1 cup sorghum flour
1 cup cocoa powder
½ cup potato starch
½ cup brown rice flour (superfine)
¼ cup arrowroot
1 tablespoon cream of tartar
1 teaspoon baking soda
1 teaspoon sea salt
½ teaspoon xanthan gum

STEP THREE (wet ingredients)
1 cup hot water
¾ cup melted coconut oil
¾ cup agave nectar
2 tablespoons mint extract
1 tablespoon vanilla extract

STEP FOUR
1 cup dark chocolate chips

STEP SIX
Chocolate Frosting *(see recipe on page 79)**
22 mint leaves (optional)
½ cup dark chocolate chips (optional)

*Note: The frosting recipe takes at least 6 hours to prepare, including freezing and refrigeration time. Plan accordingly.

Instructions

Preheat the oven to 350°F. Line muffin tins with paper liners.

STEP ONE
In a medium bowl, mix together the coconut milk and the apple cider vinegar and set aside for 5 minutes.

STEP TWO
In a separate medium bowl, sift the dry ingredients and mix them together.

STEP THREE
Add the remaining wet ingredients into the coconut milk/apple cider mixture.

STEP FOUR
Slowly add the dry mixture into the wet mixture and whisk until smooth. Stir in the dark chocolate chips. Fill each paper cupcake liner ¾ of the way full with batter.

STEP FIVE
Bake for 15 minutes. Rotate and bake for 5 more minutes. Let the cupcakes cool for 20 minutes before removing them from the pan.

STEP SIX
Once the cupcakes have completely cooled to room temperature, frost them with the prepared frosting. Garnish each with a small mint leaf and chocolate chips (optional).

MEXICAN HOT CHOCOLATE CUPCAKES

Yields 22 cupcakes

Our head baker, Ryan, came up with this twist on our chocolate cupcake and I am grateful to him for that! It is a fun way to spice up the recipe, with a subtle kick of cayenne. The addition of the cinnamon gives it an additional layer of flavor that reminds me of the perfect winter elixir. It pairs perfectly with the cooling flavor of Ryan's "Whipped Cream."

Ingredients

STEP ONE (wet ingredients)
½ cup coconut milk (carton)
2 teaspoons apple cider vinegar

STEP TWO (dry ingredients)
1¼ cups coconut sugar
1 cup sorghum flour
1 cup cocoa powder
½ cup potato starch
½ cup brown rice flour (superfine)
¼ cup arrowroot
1 tablespoon + 1 teaspoon cinnamon
1 tablespoon cream of tartar
1 teaspoon baking soda
1 teaspoon sea salt
½ teaspoon xanthan gum
½ teaspoon cayenne
½ teaspoon cloves

STEP THREE (wet ingredients)
1 cup hot water
¾ cup melted coconut oil
¾ cup agave nectar
1 tablespoon vanilla extract

STEP SIX
Ryan's "Whipped Cream" *(see recipe on page 80)**
Cinnamon (optional)

*Note: The whipped cream recipe requires at least 1 hour to make, including freezing time. Plan accordingly.

Instructions

Preheat the oven to 350°F. Line muffin tins with paper liners.

STEP ONE
In a medium bowl, mix together the coconut milk and the apple cider vinegar and set aside for 5 minutes.

STEP TWO
In a separate medium bowl, sift the dry ingredients and mix them together.

STEP THREE
Add the remaining wet ingredients into the coconut milk/apple cider mixture.

STEP FOUR
Slowly add the dry mixture into the wet mixture and whisk until smooth. Fill each paper cupcake liner ¾ of the way full with batter.

STEP FIVE
Bake for 15 minutes. Rotate and bake for 5 more minutes. Let the cupcakes cool for 20 minutes before removing them from the pan.

STEP SIX
Once the cupcakes have completely cooled to room temperature, frost them with the prepared whipped cream. Garnish with a sprinkle of cinnamon (optional).

FAUXSTESS CUPCAKES

Yields 22 cupcakes

Remember when you would see the packaged dessert section in your local convenience store (around Philadelphia that's known as a WaWa)? Well, before being diagnosed with food allergies and intolerances, and subsequently understanding how much food impacts our health, my favorite one to grab was the chocolate Hostess cupcake with the cream filling and chocolate frosting on top. Years later, once I had my allergen-free chocolate recipe down, I knew that this recipe would be close behind. The melted chocolate ganache on top really makes all the difference in the world. I love this cupcake so much that I don't even miss the chemical and allergen-filled original.

Ingredients

STEP ONE (wet ingredients)
½ cup coconut milk (carton)
2 teaspoons apple cider vinegar

STEP TWO (dry ingredients)
1¼ cups coconut sugar [Cane sugar or Palm sugar]
1 cup sorghum flour
1 cup cocoa powder
½ cup potato starch
½ cup brown rice flour (superfine)
¼ cup arrowroot
1 tablespoon cream of tartar
1 teaspoon baking soda [Bi Carb of Soda]
1 teaspoon sea salt
½ teaspoon xanthan gum [Binding agent]

STEP THREE (wet ingredients)
1 cup hot water
¾ cup melted coconut oil
¾ cup agave nectar
1 tablespoon vanilla extract

STEP SIX
Vanilla Frosting *(see recipe on page 76)**
Chocolate Ganache *(see recipe on page 83)*

Note: The frosting recipe takes at least 6 hours to prepare, including freezing and refrigeration time. Plan accordingly.

Instructions

Preheat the oven to 350°F. Line muffin tins with paper liners.

STEP ONE
In a medium bowl, mix together the coconut milk and the apple cider vinegar and set aside for 5 minutes.

STEP TWO
In a separate medium bowl, sift the dry ingredients and mix them together.

STEP THREE
Add the remaining wet ingredients into the coconut milk/apple cider mixture.

STEP FOUR
Slowly add the dry mixture into the wet mixture and whisk until smooth. Fill each paper cupcake liner ¾ of the way full with batter.

STEP FIVE
Bake for 15 minutes. Rotate and bake for 5 more minutes. Let the cupcakes cool for 20 minutes before removing them from the pan.

STEP SIX
Once the cupcakes have completely cooled to room temperature, hollow out each cupcake *(see **Cupcake Corer or Paring Knife** on page 22 for instructions on this process)* and fill them with vanilla frosting. Then dip each cupcake into the warmed chocolate ganache. Make sure the top of each cupcake is smooth. Refrigerate them until the ganache cools and becomes firm. Use a pastry bag fitted with a small round tip, to pipe on vanilla frosting in loop-de-loops on the top of each cupcake.

SALTED CARAMEL CUPCAKES

Yields 22 cupcakes

One of my most guilty pleasures used to be dark chocolate sea salt caramels from my favorite candy store in Watch Hill, Rhode Island. Our family has spent many vacations in that area, and just thinking about them can make my mouth water. This craving alone was strong enough to send me into the kitchen to come up with a healthier, allergen-free version. I found it in a cupcake. Sprinkling fleur de sel, or any quality coarse sea salt, on top is really worth the splurge if you ask me—that salty-sweet combo awakens your taste buds and leaves no craving behind!

Ingredients

STEP ONE (wet ingredients)
½ cup coconut milk (carton)
2 teaspoons apple cider vinegar

STEP TWO (dry ingredients)
1 ¼ cups coconut sugar
1 cup sorghum flour
1 cup cocoa powder
½ cup potato starch
½ cup brown rice flour (superfine)
¼ cup arrowroot
1 tablespoon cream of tartar
1 teaspoon baking soda *Bicarb of Soda*
1 teaspoon sea salt
½ teaspoon xanthan gum

STEP THREE (wet ingredients)
1 cup hot water
¾ cup melted coconut oil
¾ cup agave nectar
1 tablespoon vanilla extract

STEP SIX
Caramel Sauce *(see recipe on page 82)*
Vanilla Frosting *(see recipe on page 76)**
Chocolate Ganache *(see recipe on page 83)*
Fleur de sel or course sea salt (optional)

*Note: The frosting recipe takes at least 6 hours to prepare, including freezing and refrigeration time. Plan accordingly.

Instructions

Preheat the oven to 350°F. Line muffin tins with paper liners.

STEP ONE
In a medium bowl, mix together the coconut milk and the apple cider vinegar and set aside for 5 minutes.

STEP TWO
In a separate medium bowl, sift the dry ingredients and mix them together.

STEP THREE
Add the remaining wet ingredients into the coconut milk/apple cider mixture.

STEP FOUR
Slowly add the dry mixture into the wet mixture and whisk until smooth. Fill each paper cupcake liner ¾ of the way full with batter.

STEP FIVE
Bake for 15 minutes. Rotate and bake for 5 more minutes. Let the cupcakes cool for 20 minutes before removing them from the pan.

STEP SIX
Once the cupcakes have completely cooled to room temperature, hollow out each cupcake *(see **Cupcake Corer or Paring Knife** on page 22 for instructions on this process)* and fill them with caramel sauce. Apply a dollop of vanilla frosting on top of each cupcake. Chill the cupcakes for a few minutes and then dip the top of each cupcake in the warmed chocolate ganache. Garnish each with a small pinch of fleur de sel or coarse sea salt (optional).

APPLE CRISP CUPCAKES

Yields 16 cupcakes

I wanted to come up with a recipe that would remind me of Germany where I lived with my family for three years during my high school days. One of my favorite treats to enjoy there was Apfelkuchen, or apple cake. Finding a certified gluten-free oat (for those who can tolerate them) is crucial to this recipe, because the crumb topping is the best part. One bite of this cupcake and you'll be saying, "danke schön!"

Ingredients

STEP ONE (wet ingredients)
½ cup coconut milk (carton)
2 teaspoons apple cider vinegar

STEP TWO (dry ingredients)
1¼ cups coconut sugar *use palm sugar or cane sugar*
1 cup sorghum flour
1 cup potato starch
1 cup white rice flour
¼ cup arrowroot
¼ cup cinnamon
1½ teaspoons cream of tartar
1 teaspoon baking soda *B¹ Carb of Soda·*
1 teaspoon sea salt
½ teaspoon xanthan gum *- Binding agent·*

STEP THREE (wet ingredients)
¾ cup melted coconut oil
¾ cup maple syrup
½ cup hot water
3 tablespoons vanilla extract

STEP FOUR
1 cup shredded apples, lightly sautéed
Pinch of cinnamon

STEP FIVE (crumb topping)
1½ cups oats
¼ cup + 2 tablespoons brown rice flour
   (superfine)
6 tablespoons coconut sugar *palm sugar cane sugar*
¼ cup melted coconut oil
1½ teaspoons cinnamon
¼ teaspoon sea salt

STEP SEVEN
Vanilla Frosting *(see recipe on page 76)**
Caramel Sauce *(see recipe on page 82)*
¼ cup crumb topping from STEP FIVE

Instructions

Preheat the oven to 350°F. Line muffin tins with paper liners.

STEP ONE
In a medium bowl, mix together the coconut milk and the apple cider vinegar and set aside for 5 minutes.

STEP TWO
In a separate medium bowl, sift the dry ingredients and mix them together.

STEP THREE
Add the remaining wet ingredients into the coconut milk/apple cider mixture.

STEP FOUR
Slowly add the dry mixture into the wet mixture, whisk until smooth and set aside. In a small sauté pan, lightly sauté the shredded apples with a pinch of cinnamon for about 5 to 10 minutes. Mix the apples into the batter until evenly distributed. Fill each paper cupcake liner ¾ of the way full with batter.

STEP FIVE
In a medium bowl, mix together the crumb topping ingredients. Scoop about 1 tablespoon over each of the cupcakes. (Reserve about ¼ cup of the topping for garnish.)

STEP SIX
Bake for 15 minutes. Rotate and bake for 5 more minutes. Let the cupcakes cool for 20 minutes before removing them from the pan.

STEP SEVEN
Once the cupcakes have completely cooled, frost them with the prepared frosting. Drizzle each of the tops with caramel sauce and a sprinkle of the reserved crumb topping.

*Note: The frosting recipe takes at least 6 hours to prepare, including freezing and refrigeration time. Plan accordingly.

BANANA CHOCOLATE CHIP CUPCAKES

Yields 20 cupcakes

I knew that I needed to open Sweet Freedom with a banana chocolate chip-flavored treat, because it is one of my most favorite flavor combinations. Oddly enough, it is now one of my son Chase's favorite flavors as well—like mother like son I suppose! We gave him a small banana chocolate chip smash-cake with chocolate frosting for his first birthday. With his allergies to dairy and eggs, I am so proud that I was able to provide for him this important first birthday ritual. The photos that I have of that day with his delighted face covered in chocolate frosting will be treasured forever.

Ingredients

STEP ONE (dry ingredients)
1 ¼ cups coconut sugar *[handwritten: palm sugar or cane sugar]*
1 cup sorghum flour
1 cup potato starch
1 cup white rice flour
¼ cup arrowroot
2 teaspoons baking soda *[handwritten: is bicarby soda.]*
1 teaspoon sea salt
½ teaspoon cream of tartar
½ teaspoon xanthan gum

STEP TWO (wet ingredients)
1 cup hot water
¾ cup banana puree
¾ cup melted coconut oil
6 tablespoons agave nectar
1 tablespoon vanilla extract

STEP THREE
1 cup dark chocolate chips

STEP FIVE
Chocolate Frosting *(see recipe on page 79)**
Vanilla Frosting *(see recipe on page 76)**
20 dehydrated banana chips (optional)
¼ cup dark chocolate chips (optional)

*Note: The frosting recipe takes at least 6 hours to prepare, including freezing and refrigeration time. Plan accordingly.

Instructions

Preheat the oven to 350°F. Line muffin tins with paper liners.

STEP ONE
In a medium bowl, sift the dry ingredients and mix them together.

STEP TWO
In a separate bowl, mix together the wet ingredients.

STEP THREE
Add the dry mixture into the wet mixture and stir until smooth. Fold in the chocolate chips. Fill each paper cupcake liner ¾ of the way full with batter.

STEP FOUR
Bake for 15 minutes. Rotate and bake for 5 more minutes. Let the cupcakes cool for 20 minutes before removing them from the pan.

STEP FIVE
Once the cupcakes have completely cooled to room temperature, frost* them with the prepared frosting. Garnish each with a dehydrated banana chip and/or chocolate chips (optional).

*Note: Fill one half side of a pastry bag with chocolate frosting, and the other side with vanilla frosting to create the swirled effect.

BROWNIE SUNDAE CUPCAKES

Yields 22 cupcakes

When I was asked to appear as a competitor on the Food Network show, "Cupcake Wars," I knew I would have to come prepared with a slew of solid cupcake recipes. Sweet Freedom was only a few months old at the time, and I needed to expand my cupcake repertoire for the taping of the show. I had a decent brownie recipe that I had been working on, and so a lightbulb went off for me—why didn't I tweak the brownie recipe and put it into cupcake format with some amazing toppings. And so, the Brownie Sundae Cupcake was born. I was so lucky that it was, because I ended up using this recipe for one of the rounds of competition on the show, and I even topped it off with an allergen-free, organic maraschino cherry. It was a hit with the judges, and I'm sure it will be with you and yours too!

Ingredients

STEP ONE (dry ingredients)
1 ½ cups sorghum flour
¾ cup cocoa powder
½ cup coconut sugar
¼ cup + 2 tablespoons potato starch
3 tablespoons arrowroot
1 ½ teaspoons cream of tartar
1 ¼ teaspoons baking soda
1 teaspoon sea salt
1 teaspoon xanthan gum

STEP TWO (wet ingredients)
¾ cup + 2 tablespoons agave nectar
¾ cup unsweetened applesauce
¾ cup melted coconut oil
¾ cup hot water
1 tablespoon + 1 teaspoon vanilla extract

STEP THREE
½ cup dark chocolate chips

STEP FIVE
Chocolate Frosting *(see recipe on page 79)**
Chocolate Ganache *(see recipe on page 83)*
Ryan's "Whipped Cream" *(see recipe on page 80)***
22 organic maraschino cherries

*Note: The frosting recipe takes at least 6 hours to prepare, including freezing and refrigeration time. Plan accordingly.
**Note: The whipped cream recipe requires at least 1 hour to make, including freezing time. Plan accordingly.

Instructions

Preheat the oven to 350°F. Line muffin tins with paper liners.

STEP ONE
In a medium bowl, sift the dry ingredients and mix them together.

STEP TWO
In a separate bowl, mix together the wet ingredients.

STEP THREE
Gently fold the dry mixture into the wet mixture, stirring well to combine. Fold in the chocolate chips. Fill each paper cupcake liner ¾ of the way full with batter.

STEP FOUR
Bake for 10 minutes. Rotate and bake for 5 more minutes. Remove the cupcakes from the oven. Place them in the refrigerator until completely cooled.

STEP FIVE
Once the cupcakes have completely cooled, frost them with the prepared chocolate frosting. Add a dollop of the whipped cream to each, and then drizzle with the chocolate ganache. Top each one off with a maraschino cherry.

CARROT CAKE CUPCAKES

Yields 28 cupcakes

My mom's carrot cake was one of my most favorite things to eat when I was growing up. That cream cheese frosting was so decadent that we would lick the bowl and load extra spoonfuls onto our cake plates. When I was experimenting with recipes, this was one of the first on my list to conquer. It sounds strange, but I decided to use Bob's gluten-free all-purpose baking flour because I thought that the subtle chickpea flavor that can sometimes be detected in that flour would actually pair well with the shredded carrots and coconut. With my creamy Vanilla Frosting on top, I almost don't miss Mom's original version. Almost.

Ingredients

STEP ONE (dry ingredients)

3 cups Bob's Red Mill gluten-free
    all-purpose baking flour
1 tablespoon + 1 teaspoon baking soda
1 tablespoon cinnamon
2 teaspoons ground ginger
1½ teaspoons sea salt
1 teaspoon cream of tartar
1 teaspoon xanthan gum
½ teaspoon nutmeg

STEP TWO (wet ingredients)

1 cup agave nectar
1 cup coconut milk (carton)
2/3 cup melted coconut oil
½ cup hot water
1 tablespoon vanilla extract

STEP THREE

3 cups shredded carrots
1 cup unsweetened shredded coconut

STEP FIVE

Vanilla Frosting *(see recipe on page 76)**
½ to 1 cup shredded coconut, lightly
    toasted (optional)**

*Note: The frosting recipe takes at least 6 hours to prepare, including freezing and refrigeration time. Plan accordingly.

**Note: Put a single layer of shredded coconut on a cookie sheet and toast for about 5 minutes at 350°F until the edges are light brown.

Instructions

Preheat the oven to 350°F. Line muffin tins with paper liners.

STEP ONE

In a medium bowl, sift the dry ingredients and mix them together.

STEP TWO

In a separate bowl, mix together the wet ingredients. Slowly add the dry mixture into the wet mixture and whisk them until smooth.

STEP THREE

Gently fold in the carrots and coconut until they are evenly distributed throughout the batter. Fill each paper cupcake liner ¾ of the way full with batter.

STEP FOUR

Bake for 15 minutes. Rotate and bake for 3 more minutes. Let the cupcakes cool for 20 minutes before removing them from the pan.

STEP FIVE

Once the cupcakes have completely cooled, frost them with the prepared frosting. Garnish them with a sprinkle of toasted coconut and/or pipe on a little carrot shape with orange and green frosting (optional).

FRENCH TOAST CUPCAKES

Yields 18 cupcakes

Cupcakes for breakfast? Yes please! This is the perfect recipe for a lazy Sunday morning. When I was little, sometimes my brother Darren and I would sleep over at my Grandma and Grandpa's house. Grandpa would make us breakfast in the morning—giant pancakes and French toast. I could only eat a few bites of his huge portions at the time, and any leftovers remaining we would put outside the back door for the birds to eat. Today, whenever I taste this cupcake, I think of Grandpa, but I definitely don't have any left for the birds to enjoy!

Ingredients

STEP ONE (wet ingredients)
½ cup coconut milk (carton)
2 teaspoons apple cider vinegar

STEP TWO (dry ingredients)
1¼ cups coconut sugar
1 cup sorghum flour
1 cup potato starch
1 cup white rice flour
¼ cup arrowroot
1 tablespoon cream of tartar
1 teaspoon baking soda
1 teaspoon sea salt
½ teaspoon xanthan gum
½ teaspoon cinnamon
½ teaspoon nutmeg

STEP THREE (wet ingredients)
¾ cup melted coconut oil
¾ cup maple syrup
½ cup hot water
3 tablespoons vanilla extract

STEP SIX
Maple Frosting *(see recipe on page 79)**
Cinnamon (optional)

*Note: The frosting recipe takes at least 6 hours to prepare, including freezing and refrigeration time. Plan accordingly.

Instructions

Preheat the oven to 350°F. Line muffin tins with paper liners.

STEP ONE
In a medium bowl, mix together the coconut milk and the apple cider vinegar and set aside for 5 minutes.

STEP TWO
In a separate medium bowl, sift the dry ingredients and mix them together.

STEP THREE
Add the remaining wet ingredients into the coconut milk/apple cider mixture.

STEP FOUR
Slowly add the dry mixture into the wet mixture and whisk until smooth. Fill each paper cupcake liner ¾ of the way full with batter.

STEP FIVE
Bake for 15 minutes. Rotate and bake for 5 more minutes. Let the cupcakes cool for 20 minutes before removing them from the pan.

STEP SIX
Once the cupcakes have completely cooled, frost them with the prepared frosting. Garnish with a sprinkle of cinnamon (optional).

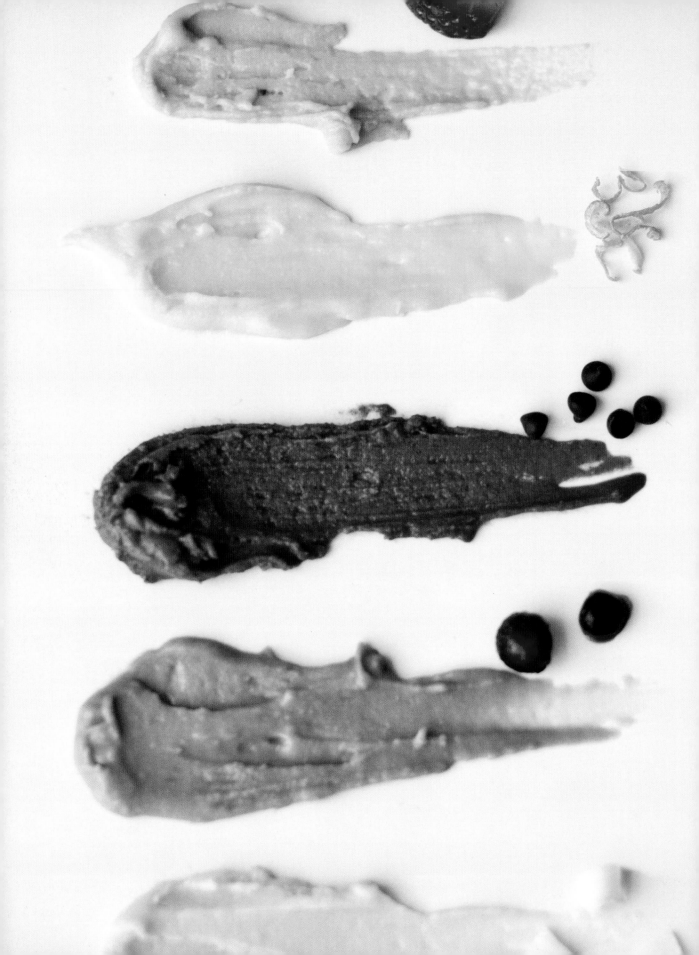

FROSTINGS, SAUCES, GLAZES, AND GANACHE

VANILLA FROSTING
Sweet Freedom's Universal Frosting Base
Yields enough to frost 48 cupcakes or four 8" cakes

I'm going to give it to you straight: Coming up with a frosting recipe that was free of dairy, eggs, gluten, soy, and common tree nuts was not easy. It took a lot of trial and error to say the least. But I finally landed on this one and I am so happy that I did. I'll be honest, though, it's not the quickest of recipes to make. It requires a bit of planning and forethought, which is something that I don't always have when a craving strikes me. And that is why this recipe makes a large batch—keep it in the freezer or fridge, depending on which stage you leave off, and you'll always be prepared. Once you get this recipe down, you'll find it really is worth the time and effort—I promise!

Ingredients

STEP ONE
2 cups coconut milk (canned, full fat)
2 cups agave nectar*
½ teaspoon sea salt

STEP TWO
3 tablespoons + 1 teaspoon arrowroot
2 tablespoons water

STEP THREE
2 cups melted coconut oil

STEP FIVE
¼ cup vanilla extract
⅛ teaspoon natural food coloring (optional)
1 ½ cups sweet rice flour (superfine)
1 cup arrowroot

If you are going to make the Maple Frosting variation (on page 79), replace the agave nectar with 1 cup of maple syrup.

Instructions

STEP ONE
In a medium saucepan, heat the coconut milk, agave nectar, and sea salt and simmer on medium heat for exactly 10 minutes.

STEP TWO
In a small bowl, combine the arrowroot and water to form a smooth paste. Begin to beat the saucepan contents with a hand mixer while slowly drizzling in the arrowroot mixture to avoid lumps forming. Continue to beat the contents of the saucepan with a hand mixer until they come briefly to a boil.

STEP THREE
Remove the saucepan from the heat and very gradually mix in the coconut oil, using the hand mixer on low to medium speed, over the course of 10 seconds. (The end result should be an even, gel-like consistency.) Transfer the frosting base to a 2-quart container and place it into the freezer until the frosting solidifies, about 4 hours or overnight. (The mixture will turn white.)

STEP FOUR
Move the container from the freezer to the refrigerator until the frosting base softens. (This will take about 2 hours in the refrigerator, or one hour at room temperature.) **Frosting flavor variations** continue from here on page 79.

STEP FIVE
To finish the vanilla frosting, mix the base until fluffy with a standing mixer or hand mixer on medium speed. Slowly add in the vanilla extract, food coloring (if using), sweet rice flour (½ cup at a time), and arrowroot (¼ cup at a time). Mix together until the frosting reaches a creamy and smooth consistency.

Note: Frosting can be stored in the refrigerator in an airtight container with a lid for several weeks, or frozen for several months until ready to thaw in the refrigerator and be used. Stirring the frosting well post-storage is recommended before using.

FROSTING FLAVOR VARIATIONS

I've included some of Sweet Freedom's most commonly used and popular frosting variations, because sometimes variety really is the spice of life. You'll find in each of our cupcake recipes the suggested frosting flavor pairing. They all begin with the Sweet Freedom Universal Frosting Base (vanilla) and end with various flavored ingredients, such as fresh juices, zests, and spices. Just because our desserts are allergen-free doesn't have to mean they're flavor-free!

All of the frostings (except for the maple frosting*), are made from the same base Vanilla Frosting recipe on page 76. Once you have completed **STEP FOUR** of the **Vanilla Frosting** recipe, follow the *instructions* for **STEP FIVE**, but *replace the ingredients* for **STEP FIVE** with these indicated below for each different flavor variation. All frostings can be stored in the refrigerator in an airtight container with a lid for several weeks, or frozen for several months until ready to thaw in the refrigerator and be used. Stirring the frosting well post-storage is recommended before using.

See note regarding Maple Frosting on page 76.

Berry Frosting

STEP FIVE (ingredients)
2 tablespoons berry extract (optional)
$\frac{1}{8}$ teaspoon natural pink or blue food coloring
$1\frac{1}{2}$ cups sweet rice flour (superfine)
1 10-oz. jar organic unsweetened berry jam

Chocolate Frosting

STEP FIVE (ingredients)
$\frac{1}{2}$ cup cocoa powder, sifted
$\frac{1}{2}$ cup sweet rice flour (superfine)

Coconut Lime Cream Frosting

STEP FIVE (ingredients)
$\frac{3}{4}$ cup lime zest
$\frac{1}{2}$ cup fresh lime juice
2 cups sweet rice flour (superfine)
1 cup arrowroot
$\frac{1}{4}$ cup shredded coconut

Eggnog Frosting

STEP FIVE (ingredients)
3 tablespoons rompopo extract
1 tablespoon vanilla extract
$\frac{1}{2}$ teaspoon nutmeg
1 pinch ground cloves
$1\frac{1}{2}$ cups sweet rice flour (superfine)
1 cup arrowroot

Lemon Cream Frosting

STEP FIVE (ingredients)
$\frac{3}{4}$ cup fresh lemon juice
$\frac{1}{2}$ cup lemon zest
2 cups sweet rice flour (superfine)
1 cup arrowroot

Maple Frosting

STEP FIVE (ingredients)
2 tablespoons vanilla extract
1 tablespoon cinnamon
$\frac{3}{4}$ cup sweet rice flour (superfine)
$\frac{1}{2}$ cup arrowroot

Mocha Frosting

STEP FIVE (ingredients)
2 tablespoons coffee extract
2 cups sweet rice flour (superfine)
$\frac{1}{2}$ cup arrowroot
$\frac{1}{2}$ cup cocoa powder, sifted

RYAN'S "WHIPPED CREAM"

Yields enough frosting for 22 cupcakes

Our head baker, Ryan, came up with this simple dessert topping that is similar to "Cool Whip" in flavor, and I'm so grateful to him for it. It's a wonderful, quicker alternative to our frostings when you're in a time pinch. One suggestion that I have is to keep a can of full-fat coconut milk in your refrigerator (unopened) at all times. That way, you can whip up some of this deliciousness whenever the mood strikes.

Ingredients

STEP ONE
2 14-oz. cans coconut milk (full fat)

STEP THREE
6 tablespoons arrowroot
6 tablespoons agave nectar
4 teaspoons vanilla extract

Instructions

STEP ONE
Chill the coconut milk in the unopened can for at least 5 hours or overnight before using. Be sure to avoid shaking the can so that the fat content stays at the top of the can.

Alternate Speed Method: Freeze the coconut milk for one hour.

STEP TWO
Open the can and scoop the solidified (white) fat from the top into a bowl, being careful not to mix in the water that has stayed below the fat.

Note: The water can be reserved for another healthy use of your choice.

STEP THREE
Whip the coconut milk fat with a hand mixer or stand mixer for one minute. Slowly add in the arrowroot and agave nectar and continue to mix on medium-high speed until the ingredients are well-combined (about a minute). Add in the vanilla extract and whip the "cream" for one final minute.

Note: After this recipe is completed, the "whipped cream" is ready for frosting immediately. However, if you would like to use a piping bag to decorate with it, chill the mixture in the fridge for an additional hour before transferring it into the piping bag to avoid it from becoming too liquid-like.)

SAUCES, GLAZES, AND GANACHE

Many of our recipes end with a little extra something on top, and that's where these lovelies come into play. You'll see throughout the cookbook where and when to use these different recipes. They are simple, short, and definitely sweet! You can store any leftover glazes in an airtight container in the refrigerator.

CARAMEL SAUCE

Yields 1 ½ to 2 cups

Ingredients

STEP ONE
1 14-oz. can coconut milk (full fat)
1 ½ cups agave nectar
6 tablespoons vanilla extract
¼ teaspoon + ⅛ teaspoon sea salt

STEP TWO
2 tablespoons + 1 ½ teaspoons arrowroot
1 tablespoon + ½ teaspoon water

Instructions

STEP ONE
In a medium saucepan over medium heat, mix together the ingredients, stirring to combine. Bring ingredients to a very gentle boil.

STEP TWO
In a separate small bowl, mix together the arrowroot and water to form a slurry. When the saucepan ingredients begin to boil, whisk in the slurry. Keep the mixture on low heat until it thickens, whisking continuously until incorporated.

CHOCOLATE GLAZE

Yields 1 cup

Follow the same recipe as for the **Chocolate Ganache** *(see page 83)*, but substitute the coconut milk with 3 tablespoons of coconut oil.

CINNAMON ROLL GLAZE

Yields enough glaze for 12 rolls

Ingredients

STEP ONE
1 14-oz. can coconut milk (full fat)
½ cup + 1 tablespoon vanilla extract
6 tablespoons agave nectar
2¾ teaspoons cinnamon
2¼ teaspoons sea salt

STEP TWO
1 tablespoon + 1 ½ teaspoons arrowroot
1 tablespoon water

Instructions

STEP ONE
In a medium saucepan over medium heat, mix together the ingredients, stirring to combine. Bring ingredients to a very gentle boil.

STEP TWO
In a separate small bowl, mix together the arrowroot and water to form a slurry. When the saucepan ingredients begin to boil, whisk in the slurry. Keep the mixture on low heat until it thickens, whisking continuously until incorporated.

LEMON GLAZE

Yields 1 ½ cups

Ingredients
STEP ONE
1 cup coconut milk (canned, full fat)
6 tablespoons lemon juice
6 tablespoons agave nectar
½ teaspoon sea salt

STEP TWO
1 tablespoon arrowroot
2 teaspoons water

Instructions
STEP ONE
In a medium saucepan over medium heat, mix together the ingredients, stirring to combine. Bring ingredients to a very gentle boil.

STEP TWO
In a separate small bowl, mix together the arrowroot and water to form a slurry. When the saucepan ingredients begin to boil, whisk in the slurry. Keep the mixture on low heat until it thickens, whisking continuously until incorporated.

ORANGE GLAZE

Yields 1 ½ cups

Follow the same recipe as for the **Lemon Glaze** above, but substitute the lemon juice with orange juice.

VANILLA GLAZE

Yields 2 cups

Ingredients
STEP ONE
1 14-oz. can coconut milk (full fat)
3 tablespoons agave nectar
3 tablespoons vanilla extract
½ teaspoon sea salt

STEP TWO
1 ½ teaspoons arrowroot
1 teaspoon water

Instructions
STEP ONE
In a medium saucepan over medium heat, mix together the ingredients, stirring to combine. Bring ingredients to a very gentle boil.

STEP TWO
In a separate small bowl, mix together the arrowroot and water to form a slurry. When the saucepan ingredients begin to boil, whisk in the slurry. Keep the mixture on low heat until it thickens, whisking continuously until incorporated.

CHOCOLATE GANACHE

Yields 1 ½ to 2 cups

Ingredients
STEP ONE
3 cups dark chocolate chips
1 cup coconut milk (carton)

Instructions
STEP ONE
In a double boiler or a medium bowl placed over a pot of water, (make sure the pot or bowl is COMPLETELY dry—any amount of water will cause the chocolate to seize), place the chocolate chips and coconut milk over medium to high heat. Stir occasionally until fully melted.

BREAKFAST GOODIES

CINNAMON ROLLS

Yields 12 rolls

Coming up with a cinnamon roll that was free of gluten, dairy, soy, eggs, corn, nuts, and other no-no's was no easy task, but a necessary one. Today, our cinnamon rolls are one of our biggest hits in the bakery, especially on Saturday and Sunday mornings. My favorite thing to do with this recipe is to make a large roll and freeze it whole. That way, I can just cut off thick "slices" to bake individually whenever I feel like it. I keep some vanilla frosting in the refrigerator so that I can easily add a dollop on top when they are warm from the oven. Make sure you add the vanilla frosting to each roll when they are still warm, so that it melts into every crevice (and in your mouth).

Ingredients

STEP ONE (dry ingredients)

1 cup potato starch
1 cup sweet rice flour
1 cup arrowroot
1 tablespoon + 1 teaspoon cream
   of tartar
1 tablespoon + 1 teaspoon xanthan gum
1 tablespoon cinnamon
1 teaspoon sea salt

STEP TWO (wet ingredients)

¼ cup melted coconut oil
1 cup coconut sugar
1⅓ cups coconut milk, (carton)
½ cup melted coconut oil
2 tablespoons vanilla extract
1 tablespoon baking soda
1 tablespoon lemon juice

STEP THREE

1 cup coconut sugar
½ tablespoon cinnamon

STEP FOUR

½ tablespoon melted coconut oil

STEP FIVE

Cinnamon Roll Glaze *(see recipe on page 82)*
Vanilla Frosting *(see recipe on page 76)**

**Note: The frosting recipe takes at least
6 hours to prepare, including freezing and
refrigeration time. Plan accordingly.*

Instructions

Preheat the oven to 350°F. Lightly oil a muffin tin with coconut oil.

STEP ONE
In a medium bowl, sift the dry ingredients and mix them together.

STEP TWO
In a separate large bowl, first combine the ¼ cup melted coconut oil and the coconut sugar and mix together. Then add the remaining wet ingredients and stir. Add the dry mixture into the wet mixture, stirring to remove any lumps. The resulting dough will be soft. In the bowl, form the dough into a round ball using your hands. Cover the bowl with plastic wrap and place it in the refrigerator for 60 minutes.

STEP THREE
Remove the dough from the refrigerator and let it rest on the counter for 15 minutes. Cover the bottom of a baking sheet with plastic wrap. In a small bowl, combine the coconut sugar and cinnamon and mix together. Sprinkle ½ tablespoon of the sugar/cinnamon mixture onto the plastic wrap. Crumble the ball of dough with your fingers and sprinkle it evenly on top of the plastic wrap. Cover the crumbled dough with another piece of plastic wrap. Press out the dough with your hands, then using a rolling pin or similar tool, roll the dough evenly into the sheet pan. Be sure to spread it to all corners.

STEP FOUR
Remove the top piece of plastic wrap. Spread a thin coat of coconut oil on the dough. Evenly distribute the sugar/cinnamon mixture across the dough's surface (reserving about 1½ tablespoons for sprinkling on top of the rolls). Use the bottom piece of plastic wrap to lift the edge of the dough. Roll the dough inward, starting at one end, forming a long cylinder shape. Place the cinnamon roll in the refrigerator for 15 minutes if baking it right away, or freeze it (wrapped airtight) for several weeks for future use.

STEP FIVE
Remove the dough from the refrigerator and slice it into 1½" wide pieces. Place the rolls (swirl side up) into the lightly oiled muffin tin. Bake the rolls for 15 minutes, remove them from the oven and let them sit for 10 minutes. Flip the rolls onto your serving dish. Top each roll with about 1 tablespoon of the cinnamon roll glaze and half of a small scoop of vanilla frosting while they are still warm. Sprinkle the tops with a dusting of the remaining sugar/cinnamon mixture.

BLUEBERRY MUFFINS
Yields 14 muffins

Blueberry muffins are a staple on the breakfast table during holidays in our house. They just seem to go so well with a nice fruit salad and a cup of hot tea. This recipe comes with a hefty portion of crumb topping too, which is just how I like to eat my blueberry muffins. When I was young, I would eat my mom's blueberry muffins with a big pat of salty butter in the middle, microwaved to melt the butter and re-warm the muffin. Now that I am healthier and more knowledgeable, I re-warm the muffins in the convection oven or toaster with a spoonful of organic coconut oil instead. They taste even better to me now!

Ingredients

STEP ONE (dry ingredients)
2 ½ cups Bob's Red Mill gluten-free
   all-purpose baking flour
1 ¼ cups coconut sugar
2 tablespoons arrowroot
1 ½ teaspoons baking soda *Bi carb Soda.*
1 teaspoon cream of tartar
½ teaspoon sea salt
½ teaspoon xanthan gum
¼ teaspoon cinnamon

STEP TWO (wet ingredients)
½ cup unsweetened applesauce
½ cup hot water
⅓ cup melted coconut oil
2 teaspoons vanilla extract

STEP THREE
1 ¼ cups frozen blueberries
¼ cup Bob's Red Mill gluten-free
   all-purpose baking flour

STEP FOUR (crumb topping)
¼ cup coconut sugar
2 tablespoons Bob's Red Mill gluten-free
   all-purpose baking flour
1 teaspoon melted coconut oil

Instructions

Preheat the oven to 350°F. Line muffin tins with paper liners.

STEP ONE
In a medium bowl, sift the dry ingredients and mix them together.

STEP TWO
In a large bowl, combine the wet ingredients. Add the dry mixture to the wet mixture, stirring until smooth.

STEP THREE
In a small bowl, toss the blueberries in flour to dust them. Gently fold the flour-dusted blueberries into the batter until they are evenly distributed. Scoop the batter into the lined muffin tins.

STEP FOUR
In a medium bowl, mix together the crumb topping ingredients. Evenly sprinkle the crumb topping onto the batter in each prepared muffin liner. Bake them for 15 minutes. Rotate and bake for 9 more minutes. Let the muffins cool for 20 minutes before removing them from the muffin tins.

CARROT LOAF

Yields 1 standard-size loaf or 15 muffins

For those who like their dessert to taste like sheer comfort food, this is a wonderful recipe to try. The carrot loaf is a great way to use up any carrots that you have hanging around your kitchen. I had to do this one summer when I participated in a vegetable farm-share and received a huge box of these root veggies. After I had pureed several batches for Chase's baby food and made some carrot cake cupcakes, what else could I do? And so, the Carrot Loaf was born. The recipe is similar to some of our other breakfast items, but with the addition of some quality spices, as well as some coconut, raisins, and a thin layer of vanilla frosting on top, the taste cannot be compared.

Ingredients

STEP ONE (dry ingredients)
1¾ cups Bob's Red Mill gluten-free all-purpose baking flour
1 cup coconut sugar
2 tablespoons arrowroot
1 tablespoon cinnamon
2 teaspoons ground ginger
1½ teaspoons baking soda *is Bi Carb of Soda!*
1 teaspoon cream of tartar
½ teaspoon sea salt
½ teaspoon xanthan gum
¼ teaspoon nutmeg

STEP TWO (wet ingredients)
2 cups shredded carrots
1 cup unsweetened shredded coconut
1 cup raisins
1 cup hot water
½ cup unsweetened applesauce
⅓ cup melted coconut oil
2 teaspoons vanilla extract

STEP FOUR
Vanilla Glaze *(see recipe on page 83)* (optional)
Vanilla Frosting *(see recipe on page 76)** (optional)

*Note: The frosting recipe takes at least 6 hours to prepare, including freezing and refrigeration time. Plan accordingly.

Instructions

Preheat the oven to 375°F. Using coconut oil, lightly oil the bottom of a standard bread loaf pan (5" x 10"), or line a muffin pan with paper liners.

STEP ONE
In a medium bowl, sift the dry ingredients and mix them together.

STEP TWO
In a large bowl, mix together the wet ingredients. Add the dry mixture to the wet mixture and stir until smooth.

STEP THREE
For loaf: Fill the prepared loaf pan with the batter and bake for 40 to 45 minutes or until a toothpick inserted in the center comes out clean.

For muffins: Fill prepared muffin tins ¾ of the way full with the batter and bake for 15 minutes. Rotate and bake for 5 more minutes.

STEP FOUR
Let the loaf or muffins cool for 20 minutes before removing them from the pan. The loaf or muffins may be topped while warm with the vanilla glaze or vanilla frosting (optional).

CINNAMON APPLE MUFFINS
Yields 1 standard-size loaf or 12 muffins

These muffins are the ultimate breakfast treat! The chunks of fresh apples really make the recipe. At the bakery, these muffins are a huge hit in the fall. Our customers come in begging for them, alongside a hot cup of our homemade apple cider. Our beloved Manager, Jen, is a whiz at restocking our cases with them when we run out, as well as shipping them to our loyal non-local followers.

Ingredients

STEP ONE (dry ingredients)
2½ cups Bob's Red Mill gluten-free
    all-purpose baking flour
1 cup coconut sugar *[OR Palm sugar OR use cane sugar]*
2 tablespoons arrowroot
1 tablespoon + 1 teaspoon cinnamon
1½ teaspoons baking soda *is Bicarb of Soda*
1 teaspoon cream of tartar
½ teaspoon sea salt
½ teaspoon xanthan gum

STEP TWO (wet ingredients)
½ cup unsweetened applesauce
½ cup hot water
⅓ cup melted coconut oil
2 teaspoons vanilla extract

STEP THREE
½ cup unpeeled apples, cut into ¼-inch
    cubes
¼ cup coconut sugar

Instructions

Preheat the oven to 350°F. Using coconut oil, lightly oil the bottom of a standard bread loaf pan (5" x 10"), or line a muffin pan with paper liners.

STEP ONE
In a medium bowl, sift the dry ingredients and mix them together.

STEP TWO
In a large bowl, combine the wet ingredients. Add the dry mixture to the wet mixture, stirring until a smooth batter is formed.

STEP THREE
Gently fold into the batter the chopped apples until they are evenly distributed. Fill the muffin tins with the batter and sprinkle the coconut sugar onto the batter in each prepared muffin liner.

STEP FOUR
For loaf: Fill the prepared loaf pan and bake for 40 to 45 minutes or until a toothpick inserted in the center comes out clean.

For muffins: Fill prepared muffin tins ¾ of the way full with the batter and bake for 15 minutes. Rotate and bake for 5 more minutes.

Let the loaf or muffins cool for 20 minutes before removing them from the pan.

LEMON POPPY SEED MUFFINS

Yields 12 muffins

Sweet Freedom's Treat-of-the-Month Club has been a big hit among our most loyal followers (near and far). Each month, Jen and our staff bake a selection of seasonal items and wrap them for shipment as soon as they are cooled from the oven. The Lemon Poppy Seed Muffin was among one of the first treats to be included in this monthly deal, and has since developed a strong following. I love this breakfast muffin with a nice portion of lemon glaze on top any time of the day (or month).

Ingredients

STEP ONE (dry ingredients)
2½ cups Bob's Red Mill gluten-free
    all-purpose baking flour
1 cup coconut sugar
¼ cup poppy seeds
2 tablespoons arrowroot
1½ teaspoons baking soda *is BiCarb of Soda*
1 teaspoon cream of tartar
½ teaspoon sea salt
½ teaspoon xanthan gum

STEP TWO (wet ingredients)
1 cup hot water
½ cup unsweetened applesauce
⅓ cup melted coconut oil
¼ cup lemon zest
2 teaspoons vanilla extract
2 teaspoons lemon extract

STEP THREE
Lemon Glaze *(see recipe on page 83)*
    (optional)
Poppy seeds (optional)

Instructions

Preheat the oven to 350°F. Line a muffin pan with paper liners.

STEP ONE
In a medium bowl, sift the dry ingredients and mix them together.

STEP TWO
In a large bowl, combine the wet ingredients. Add the dry mixture to the wet mixture, stirring until a smooth batter is formed.

STEP THREE
Fill the prepared muffin tins ¾ of the way full with the batter. Bake for 15 minutes. Rotate and bake for 5 more minutes. Let the muffins cool for 20 minutes before removing them from the pan. Top with lemon glaze and sprinkle with poppy seeds (optional).

CINNAMON SUGAR COFFEE CAKE
Yields 1 standard-size loaf

The coffee cake is a staple at breakfast in New England, and the smell of this baking in my kitchen brings me back to the breakfast table in my grandparents' house in Connecticut. Because of this fond memory, this recipe was one of the first that I developed before we opened Sweet Freedom. The concentrated cinnamon and sugar mixture in the middle of the loaf, and sprinkled on top as well, is my favorite part. I have been known to lick the cinnamon and sugar off of the spoon with this one. Yum!

Ingredients

STEP ONE (dry ingredients)
1 cup garbanzo-fava bean flour
1 cup coconut sugar
½ cup potato starch
¼ cup arrowroot
2 tablespoons cinnamon
1 teaspoon cream of tartar
1 teaspoon sea salt
¾ teaspoon baking soda *is Bicarb of Soda*
½ teaspoon xanthan gum

STEP TWO (wet ingredients)
¾ cup hot water
½ cup melted coconut oil
⅓ cup unsweetened applesauce
2 tablespoons vanilla extract

STEP THREE (swirl ingredients)
¼ cup prepared batter from STEP TWO
3 tablespoons coconut sugar *or Gran sugar or Palm sugar*
1 tablespoon cinnamon
1 tablespoon hot water

STEP FOUR
2 tablespoons coconut sugar

STEP FIVE
2 tablespoons melted coconut oil

Instructions

Preheat the oven to 350°F. Lightly oil a standard loaf pan (5" x 10") with coconut oil.

STEP ONE
In a medium bowl, sift the dry ingredients and mix them together.

STEP TWO
In a large bowl, mix together the wet ingredients. Add the dry mixture to the wet mixture and stir until a smooth batter is formed. Measure ¼ cup of the batter and set aside for use in STEP THREE. Pour the remaining batter into the prepared loaf pan.

STEP THREE
In a small bowl, mix together the swirl ingredients and stir until the mixture is creamy. Carefully drizzle the mixture down the center of the batter in the loaf pan, swirling with a spoon.

STEP FOUR
Sprinkle the top of the loaf with the coconut sugar. Bake the loaf for 24 minutes. Remove the loaf from the oven.

STEP FIVE
Brush the loaf with the coconut oil and bake for 12 more minutes. Cool the loaf for 20 minutes before removing it from the pan.

BANANA CHOCOLATE CHIP BREAD

Yields 1 standard-size loaf or 15 muffins

Oh how I love the flavor combination of bananas and chocolate. This is my favorite sweet bread to make, because it's almost foolproof, despite a few variables. The riper the bananas are, the sweeter the loaf will turn out, but any ripeness will do. One tip to keep in mind is not to heat your oil or hot water too much—the oil should just be liquid and warm, and the water should be hot but not boiling. Otherwise, you'll run the risk of melting your chocolate chips. This was the first loaf recipe we came up with at the bakery, and it is still a must-try. If you're looking for something quicker, baking them into muffin form is an easy alternative.

Ingredients

STEP ONE (dry ingredients)
1½ cups Bob's Red Mill gluten-free
    all-purpose baking flour
1 cup coconut sugar
2 tablespoons arrowroot
1½ teaspoons baking soda *is Bi Carb of Soda,*
1 teaspoon cream of tartar
½ teaspoon xanthan gum
¼ teaspoon sea salt
¼ teaspoon cinnamon

STEP TWO (wet ingredients)
1 cup pureed bananas
½ cup hot water
⅓ cup melted coconut oil
1 tablespoon vanilla extract

STEP THREE
½ cup dark chocolate chips

Instructions

Preheat the oven to 375°F. Using coconut oil, lightly oil the bottom of a standard bread loaf pan (5" x 10"), or line a muffin pan with paper liners.

STEP ONE
In a medium bowl, sift the dry ingredients and mix them together.

STEP TWO
In a large bowl, combine the wet ingredients. Add the dry mixture to the wet mixture, stirring until a smooth batter is formed.

STEP THREE
Gently fold into the batter the chocolate chips until they are evenly distributed.

STEP FOUR
For loaf: Fill the prepared loaf pan and bake for 35 to 40 minutes or until a toothpick inserted in the center comes out clean.

For muffins: Fill prepared muffin tins ¾ of the way full with the batter and bake for 15 minutes. Rotate and bake for 5 more minutes.

Let the loaf or muffins cool for 20 minutes before removing them from the pan.

ZUCCHINI BREAD

Yields 1 standard-size loaf or 15 muffins

I am so lucky that my son Chase loves his veggies. Not many little kids do, and when some of his pickier friends come over, zucchini bread is one of my favorite things to make. Zucchini has a number of nutritional benefits, including healthy doses of vitamin A and C, and a nice boost of fiber in each bite. Serving zucchini bread to the little ones is a great way to get some vegetables in, and with a little vanilla glaze on top, there's not a picky eater in the house!

Ingredients

STEP ONE (dry ingredients)
1½ cups Bob's Red Mill gluten-free
   all-purpose baking flour
1 cup coconut sugar
2 tablespoons arrowroot
1 tablespoon cinnamon
1½ teaspoons baking soda
1 teaspoon cream of tartar
½ teaspoon xanthan gum
¼ teaspoon sea salt

STEP TWO (wet ingredients)
½ cup hot water
⅓ cup melted coconut oil
2 teaspoons vanilla extract

STEP THREE
2 cups hand-grated zucchini, patted dry

STEP FOUR
Vanilla Glaze *(see recipe on page 83)*
   (optional)

Instructions

Preheat the oven to 375°F. Using coconut oil, lightly oil the bottom of a standard bread loaf pan (5" x 10"), or line a muffin pan with paper liners.

STEP ONE
In a medium bowl, sift the dry ingredients and mix them together.

STEP TWO
In a large bowl, combine the wet ingredients. Add the dry mixture to the wet mixture, stirring until a smooth batter is formed.

STEP THREE
Fold the grated zucchini into the batter, stirring until fully incorporated.

STEP FOUR
For loaf: Fill the prepared loaf pan and bake for 30 minutes or until a toothpick inserted in the center comes out clean.

For muffins: Fill prepared muffin tins ¾ of the way full with the batter and bake for 15 minutes. Rotate and bake for 5 more minutes.

Let the loaf or muffins cool for 20 minutes before removing them from the pan. While still warm, top the bread with the vanilla glaze (optional).

PLAIN DOUGHNUTS
Yields 12 doughnuts

When we introduced doughnuts into the mix at Sweet Freedom, our customers jumped for joy. So many allergy sufferers and special dieters had not touched a doughnut to their lips in years, and we didn't think that was acceptable. On weekends, our doughnuts sell out so quickly, we can barely keep them in stock. This is the plain variety, and some fun garnishes follow on the next pages to mix things up. Even though these yummies are baked and not fried, you won't be missing a thing. You'd better invest in a nice doughnut pan because these are addictive!

Ingredients

STEP ONE (wet ingredients)
1 cup coconut milk (carton)
1 teaspoon apple cider vinegar

STEP TWO (dry ingredients)
2 cups Bob's Red Mill gluten-free
    all-purpose baking flour
1 ½ cups coconut sugar
½ cup arrowroot
1 ½ teaspoons cream of tartar
¾ teaspoon baking soda
½ teaspoon sea salt

STEP THREE (wet ingredients)
½ cup melted coconut oil
¼ cup vanilla extract
2 tablespoons unsweetened applesauce

STEP FOUR
½ cup hot water

Instructions

Preheat the oven to 350°F. Lightly oil doughnut pans with coconut oil.

STEP ONE
In a medium bowl, mix together the coconut milk and the apple cider vinegar and set aside for 5 minutes.

STEP TWO
In a separate medium bowl, sift the dry ingredients and mix them together.

STEP THREE
Add the remaining wet ingredients into the coconut milk/apple cider mixture. Slowly add the dry mixture into the wet mixture and whisk them until smooth.

STEP FOUR
Mix in the hot water and whisk the batter until smooth. Fill doughnut pans with the prepared batter almost to the top. Bake them for 15 minutes. As soon as the doughnuts come out of the oven, flip them out of the pan and let them cool.

Alter the flavor and toppings for each doughnut using the **Garnishes** on page 105 (optional).

DOUGHNUT GARNISHES

Chocolate Caramel Drizzle Doughnuts

Dip the doughnuts in **Chocolate Glaze** *(see recipe on page 82)* and then drizzle them with **Caramel Sauce** *(see recipe on page 82)*. For added decadence, top them with crumbled **Chocolate Chip Cookies** *(see recipe on page 26)*.

Chocolate Glazed Doughnuts

Dip the doughnuts in **Chocolate Glaze** *(see recipe on page 82)*. Place the glazed doughnuts in the refrigerator to solidify before serving.

Cinnamon Sugar Doughnuts

In a small bowl, mix together ¼ cup coconut sugar and 2 teaspoons cinnamon and set aside. Brush each doughnut lightly with about ¼ teaspoon melted coconut oil. Then gently sprinkle them with coconut sugar/cinnamon mixture.

Lemon Coconut Doughnuts

Dip the doughnuts in **Lemon Glaze** *(see recipe on page 83)*. Put a single layer of ¼ cup shredded coconut on a cookie sheet and toast for about 5 minutes at 350°F until the edges are light brown.
Then sprinkle on top of the doughnuts.

Vanilla Glazed Doughnuts

Dip the doughnuts in **Vanilla Glaze** *(see recipe on page 83)*.

CHOCOLATE DOUGHNUTS
Yields 12 doughnuts

These are my favorite doughnuts, because they are such a classic sweet, and one of the biggest cravings I had after I had been diagnosed with food intolerances. I wasn't sure I'd ever be able to enjoy a doughnut again. Though the recipe is similar to the other doughnuts, the rich cocoa really gives them another flavor layer. This is an instance where using a good quality cocoa powder is important! I like to top these doughnuts with chocolate ganache and chocolate chip cookie crumbles—such a decadent treat!

Ingredients

STEP ONE (wet ingredients)
¾ cup coconut milk (carton)
½ teaspoon + ⅛ teaspoon apple cider vinegar

STEP TWO (dry ingredients)
1½ cups Bob's Red Mill gluten-free all-purpose baking flour
1½ cups coconut sugar
½ cup + 1 tablespoon cocoa powder
½ cup arrowroot
1 teaspoon cream of tartar
½ teaspoon baking soda
½ teaspoon sea salt

STEP THREE (wet ingredients)
6 tablespoons melted coconut oil
1 tablespoon + 1½ teaspoons unsweetened applesauce
¾ teaspoon vanilla extract

STEP FOUR
½ cup hot water

Instructions

Preheat the oven to 350°F. Lightly oil doughnut pans with coconut oil.

STEP ONE
In a medium bowl, mix together the coconut milk and the apple cider vinegar and set aside for 5 minutes.

STEP TWO
In a separate medium bowl, sift the dry ingredients and mix them together.

STEP THREE
Add the remaining wet ingredients into the coconut milk/apple cider mixture. Slowly add the dry mixture into the wet mixture and whisk them until smooth.

STEP FOUR
Mix in the hot water and whisk the batter until smooth. Fill doughnut pans with the prepared batter almost to the top. Bake them for 15 minutes. As soon as the doughnuts come out of the oven, flip them out of the pan and let them cool.

Alter the flavor and toppings for each doughnut using the **Garnishes** on page 105 (optional).

PUMPKIN DOUGHNUTS
Yields 12 doughnuts

Nothing says fall like a pumpkin doughnut. The addition of the cinnamon and spices in these doughnuts transports you instantly to the hay ride and the apple orchard. At Sweet Freedom we use the canned organic (unsweetened) pumpkin, but you can use fresh pumpkin at home if you have the time. Either way, the taste is amazing. My favorite way to enjoy these doughnuts is to top them with a cinnamon & sugar mixture. To me, this recipe paired with a glass of hot apple cider is sheer heaven!

Ingredients

STEP ONE (wet ingredients)
1 cup coconut milk (carton)
1 teaspoon apple cider vinegar

STEP TWO (dry ingredients)
2 cups Bob's Red Mill gluten-free
    all-purpose baking flour
1½ cups coconut sugar
1½ teaspoons cream of tartar
1 teaspoon cinnamon
¾ teaspoon baking soda (Bi carb of Soda)
½ teaspoon sea salt
½ teaspoon nutmeg
½ teaspoon ground ginger
½ teaspoon ground cloves

STEP THREE (wet ingredients)
¼ cup melted coconut oil
2 tablespoons organic pumpkin puree
1 teaspoon vanilla extract

STEP FOUR
½ cup hot water

STEP FIVE
Vanilla Glaze *(see recipe on page 83)*
    (optional)
¼ cup coconut sugar (optional)
2 teaspoons cinnamon (optional)
⅓ cup melted coconut oil (optional)

Instructions

Preheat the oven to 350°F. Lightly oil doughnut pans with coconut oil.

STEP ONE
In a medium bowl, mix together the coconut milk and the apple cider vinegar and set aside for 5 minutes.

STEP TWO
In a separate medium bowl, sift the dry ingredients and mix them together.

STEP THREE
Add the remaining wet ingredients into the coconut milk/apple cider mixture. Slowly add the dry mixture into the wet mixture and whisk them until smooth.

STEP FOUR
Mix in the hot water and whisk the batter until smooth. Fill doughnut pans with the prepared batter almost to the top. Bake them for 15 minutes. As soon as the doughnuts come out of the oven, flip them out of the pan and let them cool.

STEP FIVE
Drizzle vanilla glaze on the tops of the doughnuts (optional). Or as another alternative, combine the coconut sugar and cinnamon in a small bowl, lightly brush 1 teaspoon of melted coconut oil on top of each doughnut and then sprinkle on a pinch of the sugar/cinnamon mixture (optional).

CINNAMON SUGAR CRULLERS
Yields 8 crullers

I thought the cruller would be a fun way to add a different texture and dimension to our doughnut recipes. You can easily find a cruller pan online, and it's a fun addition to your baking arsenal. The recipe isn't dissimilar to the doughnut recipe, but the format is more original and unexpected. When you show up at a breakfast or brunch with a plate of crullers, everyone is sure to be wowed and impressed. Don't skimp on the cinnamon & sugar topping—it really finishes the recipe and makes it complete!

Ingredients

STEP ONE (wet ingredients)
1 cup coconut milk (carton)
1 teaspoon apple cider vinegar

STEP TWO (dry ingredients)
2 cups Bob's Red Mill gluten-free
   all-purpose baking flour
1½ cups coconut sugar
½ cup arrowroot
1 tablespoon cream of tartar
1½ teaspoons baking soda *Bi Carb of Soda*
1 teaspoon cinnamon
½ teaspoon sea salt

STEP THREE (wet ingredients)
¼ cup vanilla extract
2 tablespoons unsweetened applesauce
½ cup melted coconut oil

STEP FOUR
½ cup hot water
2 tablespoons melted coconut oil

STEP FIVE (topping ingredients)
¼ cup coconut sugar
2 teaspoons cinnamon

Instructions

Preheat the oven to 350°F. Lightly oil cruller pans with coconut oil.

STEP ONE
In a medium bowl, mix together the coconut milk and the apple cider vinegar and set aside for 5 minutes.

STEP TWO
In a separate medium bowl, sift the dry ingredients and mix them together.

STEP THREE
Add the remaining wet ingredients into the coconut milk/apple cider mixture. Slowly add the dry mixture into the wet mixture and whisk them until smooth.

STEP FOUR
Mix in the hot water and whisk the batter until smooth. Fill the cruller pans with the prepared batter almost to the top. Bake them for 17 minutes. As soon as the crullers come out of the oven, flip them out of the pan. Brush them lightly with the melted coconut oil and let them cool.

STEP FIVE
In a small bowl, mix together the coconut sugar and cinnamon. Sprinkle the tops of the crullers with the sugar/cinnamon mixture.

FESTIVE FAVORITES
and
HOLIDAY TREATS

APPLE PIE
Yields one 9" pie

Not many would dispute that the all-American holiday dessert is none other than the Apple Pie. It is a favorite in our country, and at Sweet Freedom too, especially during Thanksgiving. This is one of the few recipes in this cookbook that calls for the coconut oil to be solid (white), instead of melted (clear). The reason for this is because we are mimicking a "cutting in" method (normally achieved by cutting cold butter into a flour mixture) to achieve a light and flakey pie crust. Once you've got the crust down, the rest of the recipe is, well, easy as pie (and delicious to boot).

Ingredients

STEP ONE (dry ingredients for pie crust)
1½ cups brown rice flour (superfine)
1 tablespoon arrowroot
1 teaspoon coconut sugar *- (palm sugar, cane sugar)*
¾ teaspoon sea salt
½ teaspoon cinnamon

STEP TWO (wet ingredients for pie crust)
½ cup coconut oil, solid *canola, Rapeseed oil*
1½ tablespoons vanilla extract
3 tablespoons agave nectar
½ cup + 1 tablespoon ice cold water

STEP THREE (pie filling ingredients)
3½ to 4 cups apples, peeled and
   thinly sliced
¼ cup + 2 tablespoons coconut sugar *can use palm or cane sugar*
¼ cup coconut oil, solid
1 tablespoon vanilla extract
1 tablespoon cinnamon

STEP FOUR (crumb topping ingredients)
½ cup coconut sugar *as above*
½ cup brown rice flour (superfine)
¼ cup coconut oil, solid *Canola oil Rapeseed oil (Alt)*

STEP FIVE
Ryan's "Whipped Cream" *(see recipe on page 80)** (optional)

*Note: The whipped cream recipe requires at least 1 hour to make, including freezing time. Plan accordingly.

Instructions

Preheat the oven to 400°F. Lightly oil and then flour the bottom of a pie pan with coconut oil.

STEP ONE
In a medium bowl, sift the dry ingredients for the pie crust and mix them together.

STEP TWO
Gradually add in the solid coconut oil to the dry mixture (preferably with a standing mixer set on low). Once the mixture is crumbly, add in the vanilla extract and agave nectar. Slowly add in the water—2 tablespoons at a time. Remove the resulting dough from the bowl and form it into a ball shape with your hands. Next, flatten the dough into a round disk and place it into a pie pan. Using the heel of your hand, press the dough into the pan up along the sides to form a crust. Crimp the edges with your fingers. Place the pie crust into the refrigerator until you're ready to fill it.

STEP THREE
Meanwhile, place the pie filling ingredients into a medium skillet or saucepan. Sauté them over medium heat for about 5 to 7 minutes until the apple edges begin to brown. Remove the pie crust from the refrigerator. Spoon the sautéed apple mixture into the pie crust, mounding it in the center.

STEP FOUR
Using a fork, mix together the crumb topping ingredients in a medium bowl until they form a crumbly consistency. (If needed, add more solid coconut oil.) Cover the top of the pie with the crumb topping. Shield the edges of the pie with tin foil or pie shields.

STEP FIVE
Bake for 30 minutes. Serve with a dollop of Ryan's "Whipped Cream" (optional).

PUMPKIN PIE

Yields one 9" pie

Some people don't want to know or hear that the decadent dessert they are eating can actually be good for their health, but I am quite the opposite. I love knowing that what I'm eating won't do any major damage to my body, even though it tastes as if it will. This recipe contains the most organic (unsweetened) pumpkin puree of any of the recipes in this book, and so you can feel that you're getting a good dose of vitamins with each bite. One cup of pumpkin contains more than twice the recommended intake of vision-supporting Vitamin A and beta-carotene. Carotenoids, highly abundant in pumpkin, help to neutralize free-radicals and potentially fight cancer cells. When I was counseling my clients about their nutrition, pumpkin was one of my favorite foods to recommend to those looking for something that tastes rich and creamy while being so health-supportive at the same time.

Ingredients

STEP ONE (dry ingredients for pie crust)
1 ½ cups brown rice flour (superfine)
1 tablespoon arrowroot
1 teaspoon coconut sugar
¾ teaspoon sea salt
¼ teaspoon + ⅛ teaspoon cinnamon

STEP TWO (wet ingredients for pie crust)
½ cup coconut oil, solid
1 ½ tablespoons vanilla extract
3 tablespoons agave nectar
½ cup + 1 tablespoon ice cold water

STEP THREE (pie filling ingredients)
1 15-oz. can organic pumpkin puree
1 14-oz. can coconut milk (full fat)
2 teaspoons vanilla extract
¾ cup coconut sugar
¼ cup arrowroot
2 tablespoons potato starch
1 ½ teaspoons cinnamon
½ teaspoon sea salt
⅛ teaspoon ground ginger
⅛ teaspoon nutmeg
⅛ teaspoon cloves

(Note: The pie filling yields approximately 4 cups. You only need about 2¾ cups for this recipe. Store the remaining filling in the refrigerator to make future mini-pies!)

STEP FOUR
Ryan's "Whipped Cream" *(see recipe on page 80)* (optional)

Instructions

Preheat the oven to 400°F. Lightly oil and then flour the bottom of a pie pan with coconut oil.

STEP ONE
In a medium bowl, sift the dry ingredients for the pie crust and mix them together.

STEP TWO
Gradually add in the solid coconut oil to the dry mixture (preferably with a standing mixer set on low). Once the mixture is crumbly, add in the vanilla extract and agave nectar. Slowly add in the water—2 tablespoons at a time. Remove the resulting dough from the bowl and form it into a ball shape with your hands. Next, flatten the dough into a round disk and place it into a pie pan. Using the heel of your hand, press the dough into the pan up along the sides to form a crust. Crimp the edges with your fingers. Place the pie crust into the refrigerator until you're ready to fill it.

STEP THREE
Place the pumpkin puree, coconut milk, and vanilla into a medium bowl. Sift in the coconut sugar, arrowroot, and potato starch. Then add in the remaining ingredients. Mix the ingredients together (preferably with a standing or hand mixer) until they are incorporated. Remove the pie crust from the refrigerator. Pour 2¾ cups of the filling into the pie crust. Cover the edges of the pie crust with aluminum foil or pie shields.

STEP FOUR
Bake the pie for 30 minutes. Let it cool and then transfer it into the refrigerator to set for 4 hours before serving. Serve with a dollop of Ryan's "Whipped Cream" (optional).

BLUEBERRY OAT CRUMBLE
Yields 35 squares

The Blueberry Oat Crumble recipe reminds me of my grandmother. I developed this recipe one summer at our favorite beach town in Connecticut where she spent her summers growing up. With its ground flax, organic applesauce, and wild blueberries, you would never guess that this has so many antioxidants and health benefits, because it tastes so sinful! A good tip to try when baking this recipe is to wear a pair of rubber gloves if you have them. That way the sticky oats are easier to spread on top. Blueberry Oat Crumble is one of our best sellers at Sweet Freedom. During the summer months it's tough to make enough of it, and the same will probably be true in your home too!

Ingredients

STEP ONE (dry ingredients for cookie crust)
3 cups Bob's Red Mill gluten-free all-purpose baking flour
1¾ cups coconut sugar
¼ cup + 2 tablespoons flax meal
2¼ teaspoons xanthan gum
1½ teaspoons baking soda *vs Bi Carb Soda*
1½ teaspoons cinnamon
¼ teaspoon + ⅛ teaspoon nutmeg

STEP TWO (wet ingredients for cookie crust) *can sub oil OR Canola oil OR Rapeseed oil*
1½ cups melted coconut oil
¾ cup unsweetened applesauce
6 tablespoons maple syrup
3 tablespoons vanilla extract
1½ teaspoons sea salt

STEP THREE (fruit filling ingredients)
6 cups frozen blueberries
1 cup agave nectar
1 tablespoon + 1 teaspoon vanilla extract
¼ cup + 2 tablespoons arrowroot
¼ cup water

STEP FOUR (crumble topping ingredients)
3 cups oats
¾ cup brown rice flour (superfine)
¾ cup coconut sugar
¾ cup maple syrup
½ cup melted coconut oil
1 tablespoon + 2 teaspoons cinnamon
¼ teaspoon sea salt

Instructions

Preheat the oven to 350°F. Lightly grease a half sheet (12½" x 17½") pan or two 8" x 8" pans.

STEP ONE
In a medium bowl, sift and mix together the dry ingredients for the cookie crust.

STEP TWO
In a large bowl, mix together the wet ingredients for the cookie crust. Add the dry mixture to the wet mixture and stir them until a grainy dough is formed. Spread the dough evenly onto the bottom of the pan(s) and bake for 25 minutes. Remove from the oven and set aside.

STEP THREE
In a medium saucepan, heat the blueberries, agave nectar, and vanilla extract over medium heat. Mix the arrowroot with water in a small bowl to form a smooth paste. Slowly stir the paste into the blueberries and raise the heat until a gentle boil begins. Stir the blueberry/arrowroot mixture constantly until a thicker gel-like consistency is achieved (about 3 minutes). Remove the filling mixture from the heat and set aside.

STEP FOUR
In a medium bowl, combine the crumble topping ingredients until a slightly sticky consistency is achieved. Next, spread the blueberry filling from the previous step over the cookie crust in the pan(s) to create an even layer. Then cover entirely with the crumble topping and bake for 28 minutes.

STEP FIVE
Let cool for 20 minutes before placing the pan(s) in the refrigerator. Chill until cool. Cut bars into 2½" x 2½" pieces.

CRANBERRY ORANGE LOAF

1 standard-size loaf or 12 muffins

I came up with the basis of this recipe while I was studying one night for finals during graduate school. My stress levels were at an all-time high, and I wanted a little pick-me-up. It was fall, and so cranberries were abundant at the time. I decided to combine the cranberries that I had on hand with the citrusy flavor of orange, not dissimilar to my mother's cranberry sauce on Thanksgiving. I loved the loaf right away, and would often bake them in muffin form so that I could freeze extras to bring to class with me for a healthy study snack. If you put the batter into a loaf format, you will love the colorful outcome with each slice—this recipe is sure to add a pretty little something to your holiday table!

Ingredients

STEP ONE (dry ingredients)
2½ cups Bob's Red Mill gluten-free
    all-purpose baking flour
1 cup coconut sugar
2 tablespoons arrowroot
1½ teaspoons baking soda
1 teaspoon cream of tartar
½ teaspoon sea salt
½ teaspoon xanthan gum

STEP TWO (wet ingredients)
1 cup hot water
½ cup unsweetened applesauce
⅓ cup melted coconut oil *[handwritten: Canola oil aot Rapseed oil]*
¼ cup orange zest
2 teaspoons vanilla extract
2 teaspoons orange juice
1 cup frozen cranberries

STEP FOUR
Orange Glaze *(see recipe on page 83)*
    (optional)
Zest of 1 orange (optional)
Cranberries (optional)

Instructions

Preheat the oven to 375°F. Using coconut oil, lightly oil the bottom of a standard bread loaf pan (5" x 10"), or line a muffin pan with paper liners.

STEP ONE
In a medium bowl, sift the dry ingredients and mix them together.

STEP TWO
In a large bowl, mix together the wet ingredients (except the frozen cranberries). Add the dry mixture to the wet mixture and stir until smooth. Then gently fold in the cranberries until evenly distributed.

STEP THREE
For loaf: Fill the prepared loaf pan with the batter and bake for 40 to 45 minutes or until a toothpick inserted in the center comes out clean.

For muffins: Fill prepared muffin tins ¾ of the way full with the batter and bake for 15 minutes. Rotate and bake for 5 more minutes.

STEP FOUR
Let the loaf or muffins cool for 20 minutes before removing them from the pan. The loaf or muffins may be topped while warm with the orange glaze (optional). Garnish with orange zest and cranberries (optional).

PUMPKIN SPICE LOAF

Yields 1 standard-size loaf

This recipe reminds me of the first time we took Chase to the pumpkin patch to pick out some fresh pumpkins. He was only a little pumpkin himself, not even yet one year old. That day we brought home several pumpkins to use—some larger ones to display outside, and some smaller ones to bake with. Hence, the pumpkin spice loaf was born. At first I added a bit too much clove, and had to scale it back, as I find cloves to have a very strong flavor (a little bit goes a long way). Later I added in the chocolate chips (they are optional) and vanilla glaze on top to complete the recipe. I love that I have a dessert that brings me back to this special day, and I even have a photo of Chase wearing an orange sweater and sitting among the pumpkins as a keepsake. I hope you cherish this one in your home as well!

Ingredients

STEP ONE (dry ingredients)

1 ½ cups Bob's Red Mill gluten-free
    all-purpose baking flour
1 cup coconut sugar
2 tablespoons arrowroot
1 ½ teaspoons baking soda
1 teaspoon cream of tartar
½ teaspoon xanthan gum
½ teaspoon cinnamon
¼ teaspoon sea salt
¼ teaspoon cloves
¼ teaspoon nutmeg
¼ teaspoon ginger

STEP TWO (wet ingredients)

1 15-oz. can organic pureed pumpkin
½ cup hot water
⅓ cup melted coconut oil
2 teaspoons vanilla extract

STEP THREE

½ cup dark chocolate chips (optional)

STEP FOUR

Ryan's "Whipped Cream" *(see recipe
    on page 80)* (optional)*
Cinnamon (optional)
Vanilla Glaze *(see recipe on page 83)*
    (optional)

*Note: The whipped cream recipe requires at least 1 hour to make, including freezing time. Plan accordingly.

Instructions

Preheat the oven to 375°F. Lightly oil a standard bread loaf pan (5" x 10") with coconut oil.

STEP ONE
In a medium bowl, sift the dry ingredients and mix them together.

STEP TWO
In a large bowl, mix together the wet ingredients. Add the dry mixture to the wet mixture and stir until smooth.

STEP THREE
Fold the chocolate chips into the batter (if using). Pour the batter into the prepared loaf pan and bake for 35 to 40 minutes or until a toothpick inserted in the center comes out clean.

STEP FOUR
Let the loaf cool for 20 minutes before removing it from the pan. Once the loaf has cooled, frost with the prepared "whipped cream," and garnish with a sprinkling of cinnamon on top (optional). Alternatively, while the loaf is still warm, it can be topped with the vanilla glaze (optional)—which is a favorite here at Sweet Freedom Bakery!

BIRTHDAY CAKE
Yields 1 double-layer 8" round cake

It wouldn't be right if we didn't walk you through how to take one of our cupcake recipes and make it into a proper cake. We call this one a birthday cake, but it's great for any occasion. It might seem a bit daunting, but I promise the process is fairly simple. I sometimes like to add dark chocolate chips to this cake batter to make it a little extra special. The key is letting your cake cool completely before frosting it. Make sure you keep your frosting at room temperature or even in the refrigerator before frosting your cake. If the frosting gets too warm, it will be difficult to frost the cake because it will be too thin. I like a lot of frosting, and so I layer it on thick!

Ingredients

STEP ONE (wet ingredients)
½ cup coconut milk (carton)
2 teaspoons apple cider vinegar

STEP TWO (dry ingredients)
1¼ cups coconut sugar *use Palm Sugar or Cane Sugar*
1 cup sorghum flour
1 cup potato starch
1 cup white rice flour
½ cup arrowroot
1 tablespoon cream of tartar
1 teaspoon baking soda *is Bi carb of Soda*
1 teaspoon sea salt
½ teaspoon xanthan gum *— Binding Agent*

STEP THREE (wet ingredients)
1 cup hot water
½ cup melted coconut oil
½ cup agave nectar *is Sugar*
3 tablespoons vanilla extract

STEP FOUR
1 cup dark chocolate chips (optional)

STEP SIX
Vanilla or Chocolate Frosting *(see recipes on pages 76 and 79)*

Note: The frosting recipe takes at least 6 hours to prepare, including freezing and refrigeration time. Plan accordingly.

Instructions

Preheat the oven to 350°F. Lightly oil and flour the cake pans. Line the bottoms of the pans with parchment paper.

STEP ONE
In a medium bowl, mix together the coconut milk and the apple cider vinegar and set aside for 5 minutes.

STEP TWO
In a separate medium bowl, sift the dry ingredients and mix them together.

STEP THREE
Add the remaining wet ingredients into the coconut milk/apple cider mixture.

STEP FOUR
Slowly add the dry mixture into the wet mixture and whisk them until smooth. Stir in the chocolate chips (if using). Pour the batter into the cake pans, distributing evenly.

STEP FIVE
Bake the cake rounds for 25 to 28 minutes, or until a toothpick inserted in the center comes out clean. Let them cool for 20 minutes before carefully removing them from the pans.

STEP SIX
Once the cakes have cooled completely, place the bottom layer cake on a plate or platter. Frost the top of the cake round with a thick layer of the prepared frosting, spreading it out evenly. Then carefully place the second cake round on top of the first one. Frost generously all around the sides and then frost the top, smoothing it out evenly. Use a pastry bag and fancy tip to pipe on extra decorations (optional).

EGGNOG CUPCAKES

Yields 20 cupcakes

Nothing screams Christmas more than eggnog, and if you celebrate it, these cupcakes are a great way to feel festive on this wonderful holiday. If you've never tasted rompopo extract, now is the time to try it. Silvercloud Estates, the company who makes our all-natural (nothing artificial!) flavor extracts, has a wonderful version of this special flavoring and it truly makes the recipe. Rompopo is a festive Latin drink, and this recipe pays homage to my great grandfather's Venezuelan roots. If you're in a pinch and don't have any rompopo on hand however, you can always just substitute vanilla extract, making it a total of 3 tablespoons of vanilla extract. I promise the cupcakes will still taste like holiday heaven!

Ingredients

STEP ONE (wet ingredients)
½ cup coconut milk (carton)
2 teaspoons apple cider vinegar

STEP TWO (dry ingredients) _Can use Palm Sugar or Cane Sugar_
1¼ cups coconut sugar
1 cup sorghum flour
1 cup potato starch
1 cup white rice flour
½ cup arrowroot
1 tablespoon cream of tartar
2 teaspoons cinnamon
1½ teaspoons nutmeg
1 teaspoon baking soda _is Bicarb of Soda._
1 teaspoon sea salt
½ teaspoon xanthan gum
¼ teaspoon cloves

STEP THREE (wet ingredients)
1 cup hot water
½ cup melted coconut oil
½ cup maple syrup
2 tablespoons rompopo extract (optional)
1 tablespoon vanilla extract

STEP SIX
Eggnog Frosting *(see recipe on page 79)**
2 tablespoons cinnamon (optional)
1 tablespoon nutmeg (optional)

Note: The frosting recipe takes at least 6 hours to prepare, including freezing and refrigeration time. Plan accordingly.

Instructions

Preheat the oven to 350°F. Line muffin tins with paper liners.

STEP ONE
In a medium bowl, mix together the coconut milk and the apple cider vinegar and set aside for 5 minutes.

STEP TWO
In a separate medium bowl, sift the dry ingredients and mix them together.

STEP THREE
Add the remaining wet ingredients into the coconut milk/apple cider mixture.

STEP FOUR
Slowly add the dry mixture into the wet mixture and whisk them until smooth. Fill each paper cupcake liner ¾ of the way full with batter.

STEP FIVE
Bake for 15 minutes. Rotate and bake for 3 more minutes. Let the cupcakes cool for 20 minutes before removing them from the pan.

STEP SIX
Once the cupcakes have completely cooled to room temperature, frost them with the prepared frosting. In a small bowl mix the cinnamon and nutmeg together and sprinkle on top of the cupcakes (optional).

COCONUT RASPBERRY THUMBPRINTS

Yields 16 cookies

The thumbprint cookie is one of my all-time favorites. I am typically a chocoholic, but I could eat a whole batch of these cookies in one sitting. At Sweet Freedom, in order to make them feel more festive for special occasions, we roll each raw cookie in shredded coconut. The resulting cookie is such a pretty one—I think it's the perfect addition to a holiday cookie exchange. For fun, don't tell anyone that these thumbprints are free of gluten, dairy, soy, eggs, corn, refined sugars, or anything artificial. I guarantee they won't even be able to tell.

Ingredients

STEP ONE (dry mixture ingredients)
1 cup + 6 tablespoons brown rice flour (superfine)
¾ cup garbanzo-fava bean flour
¼ teaspoon baking soda *vs Bicarb y Soda*
¼ teaspoon cream of tartar
¼ teaspoon sea salt

STEP TWO (wet mixture ingredients)
1 cup + 2 tablespoons coconut sugar *can use palm sugar or cane sugar*
½ cup melted coconut oil
1 tablespoon vanilla extract
½ cup coconut milk (carton)

STEP THREE
¾ cup unsweetened shredded coconut

STEP FOUR
1 10-oz. jar unsweetened raspberry jam
Coconut sugar (for sprinkling garnish)

Instructions

Preheat the oven to 375°F. Line a sheet pan or cookie sheet with parchment paper.

STEP ONE
In a large bowl, sift the dry ingredients and mix them together.

STEP TWO
In a large bowl (preferably a standing mixer), combine the coconut sugar, coconut oil, and vanilla extract. Then add in the dry mixture and the coconut milk alternately, a little at a time until well-combined.

STEP THREE
Using an ice cream scoop or similar tool, shape the cookie dough into balls and roll each one in the shredded coconut. (It is helpful to dip the scoop occasionally in water to avoid too much of the dough sticking to the scoop.) Then place the balls onto the prepared baking sheets about 3 inches apart.

STEP FOUR
Using the back of the scoop or your thumb, make a deep indentation in the center of each cookie. Fill each indentation with a heaping teaspoon of raspberry jam and sprinkle the edges with additional coconut sugar.

STEP FIVE
Bake the cookies for 7 minutes. Rotate and bake for 5 additional minutes.

GINGERSNAPS

Yields 17 cookies

No holiday season is complete without a gingersnap cookie. I love it when we pull out the molasses in the late fall, and roll up our sleeves to begin making this festive favorite. These cookies have such a distinct flavor that they are like no other. And what makes them even better is that you're also getting a healthy dose of B vitamins and iron, thanks to the quality molasses that we use at Sweet Freedom. If eating these cookies is equivalent to taking a multivitamin, I am going to live forever!

Ingredients

STEP ONE (dry ingredients)
1¾ cups Bob's Red Mill gluten-free
   all-purpose baking flour
¾ cup coconut sugar
¼ cup flax meal
1½ teaspoons xanthan gum
1½ teaspoons ground ginger
1 teaspoon cinnamon
½ teaspoon baking soda *is Bicarb of Soda*
½ teaspoon cream of tartar
½ teaspoon sea salt
⅛ teaspoon cloves

STEP TWO (wet ingredients)
½ cup melted coconut oil
½ cup gluten-free molasses
1 tablespoon vanilla extract

STEP THREE (sugar coating)
6 tablespoons coconut sugar
1½ teaspoons cinnamon

Instructions

Preheat the oven to 350°F. Line a cookie sheet with parchment paper.

STEP ONE
In a medium bowl, sift the dry ingredients and mix them together.

STEP TWO
In a large bowl, mix together the wet ingredients. Add the dry mixture to the wet mixture and stir them until a grainy dough is formed.

STEP THREE
In a separate small bowl, mix together the sugar coating ingredients. Using an ice cream scoop or similar tool, shape the dough into round balls and roll them in the cinnamon/sugar mixture to coat fully. Place them on the cookie sheet 1 inch apart. Press down with a spoon to almost totally flatten each cookie.

STEP FOUR
Bake the cookies for 9 minutes. Rotate and bake for 4 more minutes.

PUMPKIN COOKIES

Yields 28 cookies

When I developed this recipe, I brought them over to my friend's house to share. I didn't tell anyone that they were free of all of the usual no-no's. Within minutes the whole plate was gone and I knew I was onto something. To this day, I still love the reaction from people who don't know that our treats are allergen-free. It is the biggest compliment that I can get when they tell me that Sweet Freedom desserts taste like "normal" sweets.

Ingredients

STEP ONE (dry ingredients)
2 cups Bob's Red Mill gluten-free
   all-purpose baking flour
1¾ cups coconut sugar
¼ cup flax meal
2 teaspoons cinnamon
1½ teaspoons xanthan gum
1 teaspoon baking soda
1 teaspoon sea salt
¼ teaspoon nutmeg
¼ teaspoon allspice
⅛ teaspoon ground ginger

STEP TWO (wet ingredients)
1 cup unsweetened pumpkin (canned)
¾ cup melted coconut oil
2 tablespoons maple syrup
2 tablespoons vanilla extract

STEP THREE
1 cup dark chocolate chips (optional)

Instructions

Preheat the oven to 350°F. Line a cookie sheet with parchment paper.

STEP ONE
In a medium bowl, sift the dry ingredients and mix them together.

STEP TWO
In a large bowl, mix together the wet ingredients. Using a rubber spatula, add the dry mixture to the wet mixture and stir them until a grainy dough is formed.

STEP THREE
Gently fold in the chocolate chips (if using) until they are evenly distributed throughout the dough. Using an ice cream scoop or similar tool, scoop the batter onto the prepared cookie sheet 1 inch apart. Slightly flatten the cookies. (It is helpful to dip the scoop occasionally in water to avoid too much dough sticking to the scoop.)

STEP FOUR
Bake the cookies for 9 minutes. Rotate and bake for 3 additional minutes.

SUGAR COOKIES
Yields 12 cookies

Our first holiday season at Sweet Freedom we were without a sugar cookie recipe, and I didn't find that acceptable. I just hadn't had the time to develop the recipe that year. So, for our second year in business I made it a priority to create these cookies, and I'm so glad that I did. I would make a batter through trial-and-error, bake a few cookies, let my husband, Jon, try them, and tweak the batter as needed. Luckily it only took three batches and the cookies were just right. I like to decorate them with different colored frostings, and allergen-free candies from naturalcandystore.com. These cookies are a fun and safe activity to do with kids, and will definitely help create a memorable holiday for all.

Ingredients

STEP ONE (wet mixture ingredients)
½ cup coconut oil, solid
¾ cup coconut sugar
¼ cup unsweetened applesauce
1 tablespoon vanilla extract

STEP TWO (dry mixture ingredients)
1¾ cups Bob's Red Mill gluten-free
   all-purpose baking flour
½ teaspoon baking soda
½ teaspoon cream of tartar
½ teaspoon xanthan gum
¼ teaspoon sea salt

Instructions

Preheat the oven to 350°F. Line a sheet pan or cookie sheet with parchment paper.

STEP ONE
In a medium bowl (preferably a standing mixer set on medium), combine together the solid coconut oil and the coconut sugar. Once incorporated, add in the applesauce and the vanilla extract.

STEP TWO
In a separate bowl, sift the dry mixture ingredients and mix them together.

STEP THREE
Add the dry mixture into the wet mixture and stir them until well-combined. Once all ingredients are incorporated, form the batter into a ball shape with your hands. (If the dough is too sticky to handle, then coat the dough and your hands with a little all-purpose flour or place the dough into the refrigerator to solidify for 10 minutes.)

STEP FOUR
On a piece of parchment paper, roll out the dough into a thin sheet (¼ inch thick). Using cookie cutters, cut out shapes and place them onto the lined cookie sheet. (If you have trouble rolling the dough out, place the dough ball into the refrigerator to solidify for 30 minutes, or the freezer for 15 minutes, until it is firm enough to be rolled out.)

STEP FIVE
Bake the cookies for 9 minutes. Rotate and bake them for 2 additional minutes, or until they turn golden brown. Allow the cookies to cool fully before decorating them with frosting or toppings of your choice *(see Approved Sweet Freedom Bakery Suppliers list on page 136 for ideas)*.

Approved Sweet Freedom Bakery Suppliers

Authentic Foods
www.authenticfoods.com
For superfine brown rice flour, superfine white rice flour, superfine sweet rice flour, and other allergen-free products

Bob's Red Mill
www.bobsredmill.com
For gluten-free all-purpose baking flour, ground flax, arrowroot, potato starch, flax meal, and more

Tropical Traditions
www.tropicaltraditons.com
For expeller-pressed coconut oil

Xylitol USA
www.xylitolusa.com
For coconut sugar and other natural sweeteners

TIC Gums
www.ticgums.com
For xanthan gum

Omega Nutrition
www.omeganutrition.com
For expeller-pressed coconut oil

Organic Nectars
www.organicnectars.com
For agave nectar

Seelect Tea
www.seelecttea.com
For natural food coloring

Silver Cloud Estates
www.silvercloudestates.com
For all-natural extracts and spices

Enjoy Life Foods
www.enjoylifefoods.com
For allergen-free chocolate chips

Thai Kitchen
www.thaikitchen.com
For organic, canned, unsweetened coconut milk

So Delicious
www.sodeliciousdairyfree.com
For unsweetened coconut milk from the carton

Frontier
www.frontiercoop.com
For organic spices

Flavorganics
www.flavorganics.com
For allergen-free extracts

Cocoa Supply
www.cocoasupply.com
For royal mahogany, 22/24 fat content, Dutch-alkalized cocoa powder by Bergenfield and others

Bragg
www.bragg.com
For apple cider vinegar

Other Resources

Whole Foods Market

www.wholefoodsmarket.com
If you happen to have a Whole Foods Market near you, you are in luck. Most, if not all, of the ingredients we use and recommend are sold there.

Natural Food Stores

www.organicstorelocator.com
If you do an online search for your local area, chances are you'll find a natural food store that will carry many of the ingredients we use.

Local Farmer's Markets and Farms

www.localharvest.org
Use this site to find the freshest, in-season produce, spices, jams, and more, in your local area.

Amazon

www.amazon.com
Amazon has an impressive supply of allergen-free ingredients, and many of the brands we use and recommend. Shipping is often free (and fast!) if you have a membership, and you can buy in bulk to save.

Natural Candy Store

www.naturalcandystore.com
This site has a wonderful selection of allergen-free candies and toppings to add to your decorating pantry. We love their products, especially around the holidays.

Allergy and Health-Related Resources

Allergic Girl Resources
www.allergicgirlresources.com

American Celiac Disease Alliance
www.americanceliac.org

Attention Deficit Disorder Association
www.add.org

Autism Research Institute
www.autism.com

Autism Speaks
www.autismspeaks.org

Food Allergy Education Network
www.foodallergyednetwork.org

Food Allergy Research & Education (FARE)
www.foodallergy.org

Food Allergy & Anaphylaxis Network for Kids (FAAN Kids)
www.fankids.org

Institute for Integrative Nutrition
www.integrativenutrition.com

International Foundation for Functional Gastrointestinal Disorders
www.iffgd.org

Kids With Food Allergies Foundation
www.community.kidswithfoodallergies.org

National Foundation for Celiac Awareness
www.celiaccentral.org

The Vegetarian Resource Group— Veganism in a Nutshell
www.vrg.org/nutshell/vegan.htm

Weston A. Price Foundation
www.westonprice.org/digestive-disorders/ food-allergies

Acknowledgments

With thanks and gratitude . . .

To my parents who are my biggest cheerleaders always—I love you.

To my extended family and friends who are not only the best Sweet Freedom customers and taste-testers, but who encourage me and motivate me daily. Especially to Jonathan, my sweet Chase, and our precious twin daughters, Juliet and Emmelyn, for making my life complete.

To the amazing Sweet Freedom Team, without whom this bakery and cookbook wouldn't exist. A special thank you to my Manager, Jen Kremer, for not only coming to my rescue during my time of need, but never ceasing to amaze me with all that you are capable of. Thank you for being a pleasure to work with. To our Head Baker, Ryan Hatt, for your tireless efforts and enthusiasm daily, and for coming up with fun twists on new recipes, especially your delicious Whipped Cream! And thank you to the rest of the staff—past and present—for your hard work and dedication in "baking" so many "happy" every day. Thank you to Heather Esposito for your contributions and efforts during the formation and first two years at Sweet Freedom. I appreciate each of you who has stood behind the counter at Sweet Freedom more than you know.

A special thanks to Charleen Davis, my first editor and proofreader, for your careful and thoughtful contributions to this book. To Mara Conlon and Peter Pauper Press, for "discovering" this book and validating its importance, and for giving it a platform and national voice. I'm so excited that through your efforts, *Baking You Happy* will be able to reach so many who can use and appreciate Sweet Freedom Bakery desserts. Thank you, Mara, for being so wonderful to work with!

Thank you to my amazingly talented photographer, Rachel McGinn, for producing exactly what I had envisioned. Thank you also to Beka Rendell for your expertise and beautiful style. You were both instrumental in capturing the essence of Sweet Freedom and making this cookbook come to life!

Lastly, to our loyal customers, followers, and Kickstarter contributors. Your enthusiasm and support make this all have meaning. Thank you for not only understanding how difficult it is to make allergen-free products, but for appreciating what we do by buying our treats (and now baking them at home!) and spreading the word. Being able to provide for a growing need and put a smile on your faces is both humbling and an honor. We at Sweet Freedom live to serve YOU!

Index

HOW TO CONTACT
Sweet Freedom Bakery

SWEET FREEDOM BAKERY
1424 South Street
Philadelphia, PA 19146
Phone: (215) 545-1899

SWEET FREEDOM BAKERY
1039 A W. Lancaster Avenue
Bryn Mawr, PA 19010
Phone: (610) 527-7323

SWEET FREEDOM BAKERY
577 Haddon Avenue
Collingswood, NJ 08108
Phone: (856) 869-7322

www.sweetfreedombakery.com
sweetfreedombakery@gmail.com
www.facebook.com/SweetFreedomBakery
http://pinterest.com/bakingyouhappy
https://twitter.com/sfbakery

Don't feel like baking after all? Need some further inspiration?
Order Sweet Freedom desserts online to be shipped right to you at home!

http://store.sweetfreedombakery.com/